Anger Kills

"*I'm <u>very</u> angry. What do you suggest?*"

ANGER KILLS

Seventeen Strategies for Controlling the Hostility That Can Harm Your Health

■

REDFORD WILLIAMS, M.D.,
AND
VIRGINIA WILLIAMS, PH.D.

TIMES ⚎ BOOKS

RANDOM HOUSE

Grateful acknowledgment is made to the following for permission to reprint
previously published material:

MEYER FRIEDMAN: Excerpts from *Treating Type A Behaviour—and Your Heart* by
Meyer Friedman. Copyright © 1984 by Meyer Friedman. Reprinted by permission
of the author.

VIKING PENGUIN, A DIVISION OF PENGUIN USA, INC.: "Antigone" from *Three
Theban Plays* by Sophocles, translated by Robert Fagles. Translation copyright ©
1982 by Robert Fagles. Reprinted by permission of Viking Penguin, a division of
Penguin USA, Inc.

Library of Congress Cataloging-in-Publication Data
Williams, Redford B.
Anger kills: seventeen strategies for controlling the hostility that can harm your
health / Redford Williams, Virginia Williams.
p. cm.
Includes index.
ISBN 0-8129-1981-5
1. Coronary heart disease—Psychosomatic aspects. 2. Coronary
heart disease—Prevention. 3. Anger—Health aspects. 4. Hostility
(Psychology)—Health aspects. I. Williams, Virginia Parrott.
II. Title.
RC685.C6W547   1993   616.1'2308—dc20   92-50502

Manufactured in the United States of America
9   8   7   6   5   4   3

FOR JENNIFER AND LLOYD

ACKNOWLEDGMENTS

Participants in our workshops on controlling hostility have helped to forge the final form of many of our strategies. Their commitment, energy, good ideas, sharing of personal experiences, and ability to identify what didn't work have contributed greatly to our book.

We also wish to recognize the following individuals, each of whom provided concrete help that became directly incorporated into our book: Barbara Berryman for keeping us informed about current events relating to anger; Susan Boos, who on many occasions helped to get manuscripts copied and sent off; Nicholas Gottlieb, director of "Mrs. Cage"; Margaret Harrell for her thoughtful and intelligent reading of the entire manuscript; Jim Henry as a source of ideas about brain mechanisms; Linda Jackson for keeping track of so many details; Berton Kaplan for alerting us to new points of view from the combined perspective of a humanist and scientist; Elva Parrott for her thorough research of biblical allusions to anger; Peter Smith for much help with the mechanics of permissions and other logistical problems; and Paul Stessel for contributions to the humor chapter.

The research findings presented in our book are based on the work of many scientists. Redford would like to mention for special recognition the contributions of John Barefoot, Jim Blumenthal, Margaret Chesney, Grant Dahlstrom, Ted Dembroski, Shin Fukudo, Cynthia Kuhn, Jim Lane, Dan Mark, Karen Matthews, Hirokasu Monou, Motoyasu Muranaka, Saul Schanberg, Ilene Siegler, and Ed Suarez.

Generous support for Redford's research has come from the National Institute of Mental Health and the National Heart, Lung, and Blood Institute.

In addition to being a first-rate agent, Reid Boates made important substantive contributions to the initial structuring of our manuscript.

Betsy Rapoport has lived up to her reputation as science editor par excellence.

We gratefully thank all of these people.

CONTENTS

PART IV
DEALING WITH HOSTILE PEOPLE

INTRODUCTION:

Anger Kills

Anger kills. We're speaking here not about the anger that drives people to shoot, stab, or otherwise wreak havoc on their fellow humans. We mean instead the everyday sort of anger, annoyance, and irritation that courses through the minds and bodies of many perfectly normal people.

- If your immediate impulse when faced with everyday delays or frustrations—elevators that don't immediately arrive at your floor, slow-moving supermarket lines, dawdling drivers, rude teenagers, broken vending machines—is to blame somebody;

- If this blaming quickly sparks your ire toward the offender;

- If your ire often manifests itself in aggressive action;

then, for you, getting angry is like taking a small dose of some slow-acting poison—arsenic, for example—every day of your life. And the result is often the same: Not tomorrow, perhaps, or even the day after, but sooner than most of us would wish, your hostility is more likely to harm your health than will be the case for your friend whose personality is not tinged by the tendencies to cynicism, anger, and aggression just described.

For your nonhostile friend, becoming angry when "mistreated" by others is relatively harmless—he or she becomes upset only when *really* mistreated and, even then, his or her blood pressure *doesn't* go through the roof. But for you, anger is a constant companion every day of your life, and each outburst is accompanied by a large rise in blood pressure. And that's only one health-related consequence of your anger. Anger is a toxin to your body.

Our knowledge of the health consequences of hostility and what can be done to lessen your risks stems from two sources: research carried out by Redford and many others, and our experience as a couple for more than thirty years. Indeed, many of the anger-stopping ideas we now prescribe in workshops and seminars were first tested in the research "laboratory" of our home and marriage.

Rather than the typical collaboration between two research scientists, this book reflects the interplay between Redford's research on hostility and our joint experience as a couple with one hostile partner.

Redford has spent his entire professional life pursuing research aimed at understanding how the impact of the mind and emotions upon the body can lead to serious medical illness, even death. A Yale-trained internist with two years' research experience at the National Institute of Mental Health, Redford has been on the faculty at Duke University Medical Center for the past twenty years. He is currently a professor of psychiatry, an associate professor of medicine, and the director of the Behavioral Medicine Research Center.

Over the past two decades, Redford's research has centered on Type A behavior—the kind exhibited by people who are tense, driven, competitive, hostile. It was long believed that having a Type A personality disposed you to heart disease or other illness. Redford's work demonstrated that of the several components of the Type A behavior pattern, only one—hostility—is harmful to health.

In 1989 he described the research on hostility as a serious threat to health in *The Trusting Heart: Great News About Type A Behavior*. In addition to providing the scientific evidence that hostility harms health, Redford outlined in *The Trusting Heart* a series of strategies designed to help soften hostile tendencies.

Since the publication of *The Trusting Heart,* many readers have asked for a more extensive and detailed description of these strategies for subduing their cynicism, anger, and aggression. In addition, the research evidence indicting hostility as a threat to health continues to mount. For example, very recent research conducted by Redford and others at Duke and elsewhere shows that hostile persons are also more likely to be smokers, to drink more alcohol, and to consume more calories—all habits that can seriously harm your health.

This research continues today at many institutions around the world, and further on in this book we will provide more details about the latest results. But these research findings are only part of the story we want to tell.

While Redford was learning all about the dire health consequences of hostility, we were also living our life together. As Redford learned more about hostility in his research, he began to realize that he possessed many of the personality traits characterizing those hostile people in his scientific investigations. Because he was finding that many hostile people went on to suffer serious health problems, he concluded that he would also be at risk unless he reduced his hostility.

Redford's health wasn't the only thing at risk; his hostility was causing our relationship to deteriorate, despite Virginia's increasingly assertive demand that he behave differently. Until the early 1980s, Redford frequently became angry with Virginia, as well as with the plumber, other drivers, and whoever or whatever else crossed his path. He usually first fussed with Virginia or whoever else had "messed up," then stewed, and finally sallied forth to correct whatever he perceived as the problem. Although Virginia is a "low hostile," her most usual reactions to Redford's anger were to make some cutting remarks or to become insulted, sulk, and then withdraw.

Psychotherapy helped us both, but what was most effective was our commitment to wanting to treat each other well and our wish that our marriage be a joyful and sustaining experience for ourselves and our two children. This meant that Virginia has needed to become more assertive, and Redford has needed to become less hostile.

Over the years, we have indeed made this happen. However, our behavior can lapse—Redford still sometimes rages against others' perceived incompetence and has hostile outbursts, and Virginia remains an expert at martyred sulking. Still, by applying what we preach in this book, we have learned over the years how to treat each other well most of the time. All in all, we are happy.

Unfortunately, being a hostile personality and not being assertive enough when dealing with hostile people are not personality traits you can overcome once and for all. Your basic personality type, including what may be a biological predisposition, isn't likely to change. However, what you and your intimates can learn is to recognize when you first become angry and then early on to cut off experience of this anger. You can also improve in general your relationships with other people by systematically applying principles of behavior modification. You can also make your life a more positive and joyful experience.

We have found that conquering hostility requires an ongoing lifetime commitment. Every time we find ourselves in a novel situation, Redford has to learn how to control his hostility and Virginia has to figure out how to be more assertive. In later chapters of this book, we will share with you some of these experiences from over the entire course of our adult lives.

Our most recent opportunities to practice what we preach center on the writing of this book, the biggest challenge to our marriage of the past decade. We now realize that we began with different unconscious assumptions. Virginia, an historian who wrote *Surrealism, Quantum Philosophy and World War I,* saw herself as an equal partner in this new enterprise. Redford, who has directed numerous research projects, saw himself as once again director. As we came to realize our differences of perspective, often each felt disgusted with the other and the whole undertaking. In paragraph after paragraph, chapter after chapter, we have had to deal anew with issues of listening, empathy, tolerance, assertion, and trust.

Working together on this book has, at times, made us feel as though we were starting over on the process of controlling hostility. But slowly, sometimes painfully, we have been able to learn to treat each other well while writing a book together. Listening to each other's ideas, sharing decision making, and compromising have resulted in a better book. Our marriage is also stronger, as we now have another interest in common as well as new experiences in hostility control. If *we* can succeed in controlling hostility, given our hostile and nonassertive personalities, so can you!

Before beginning, let's dispel some myths about expressing anger. Carol Tavris, in her comprehensive study, *Anger: The Misunderstood Emotion,* corrects some common misconceptions:

MYTH #1: "Aggression is the instinctive catharsis for anger."

REALITY: Aggression is an acquired cathartic habit, a learned reaction practiced by people who think they can get away with behaving this way.

MYTH #2: "Talking out anger gets rid of it—or at least makes you feel less angry."

REALITY: A series of studies indicates that overt expression can focus or even increase anger. Tavris suggests that before speaking out, evaluate whether one wants to stay angry or not.

MYTH #3: "Tantrums and other childhood rages are healthy expressions of anger that forestall neuroses."

REALITY: Tantrums, which peak at two and three years of age, begin to wane by age four, unless the child learns to control others through such behavior. As Tavris states, "The emotions are as subject to the laws of learning as any other behavior."

Another myth is that conquering hostility requires a personality wipeout. One especially flagrant (though not isolated) example can be found in the 1991 movie *Regarding Henry*. As the movie begins, the title character is portrayed as an angry and insensitive New York attorney. By the end of the movie, he has learned to shower his family with affection, has acquired a puppy, and has conquered his hostility. These changes certainly sound desirable, but we are troubled by this "magic bullet" misconception of overcoming hostility.

You see, Henry gets his newfound trusting heart only after he is shot in the head during a holdup. His memory has been deleted, and therefore Henry's physical therapist and family must retrain him from scratch. After the shooting, he has to work incredibly hard simply to perform the minimal activities of daily life, but conquering his hostility seems easy and almost effortless. In reality, conquering your hostility requires commitment, skills acquisition, and practice—but not a lobotomy!

With movie heroes like Henry, no wonder you may have misinformed misgivings about reducing anger. But fear not, for in reality you will find that you can surrender your rage without sacrificing any of your spirit.

Although controlling your hostility is neither simple nor easy—few really worthwhile accomplishments ever are—you can master the requisite skills. The physiology and upbringing of non-hostile people predispose them to healthy behaviors naturally, but hostile persons must develop skills to counter their natural tendencies. Control of hostility takes time and effort, but progress *is* possible.

- You can learn to behave more kindly toward other people and, in the bargain, predispose them to treat you better, too.

- You can learn to rein in your anger before you lose control, to shorten the list of situations that arouse your ire.

- With continuing practice, you can eventually change your cynical perceptions of others.

First you need to determine if you are at risk. In part I you will evaluate your own hostility, beginning with a questionnaire. We then turn to more subtle, individualized ways you can measure your hostility levels.

In part II, you will review the scientific evidence for our assertion that anger kills.

Most of the book focuses on conquering hostility. In part III, we start with guidance in how to *think effectively,* to reason with yourself (chapter 3). You will learn ways to try to talk yourself out of being angry if your anger is petty or unjustified and when you have no effective options for changing the situation.

Next comes a group of strategies—thought stopping (chapter 4), distraction (chapter 5), and meditation (chapter 6)—that will help you cope with situations in which you are angry but don't want to be. Basically, these are strategies to *deflect* your cynical thoughts and reduce your anger, thereby decreasing the intensity of your fight-or-flight response. You will also be reminded of ways to avoid overstimulation (chapter 7).

At times, you really are being mistreated, probably by some other hostile person. In such situations, you need to *act effectively* to take some steps to make that person stop. The chapter on assertion (chapter 8) teaches you how.

Another group of strategies—caring for pets (chapter 9), listening (chapter 10), practicing trust (chapter 11), taking on community involvement (chapter 12), increasing empathy (chapter 13), being tolerant (chapter 14), forgiving (chapter 15), and having a confidant (chapter 16)—have as their goal *improving relationships* and thereby increasing your social support. Besides teaching you how to reduce your tendencies to respond aggressively toward others, these strategies are designed specifically to increase your "connectedness" to others.

The last group of strategies—using humor (chapter 17), being religious (chapter 18), and pretending that today is your last (chapter 19)—will help you to *adopt positive attitudes* and thereby reduce your hostility by creating a more positive philosophical focus in your life.

Although we devote a separate chapter to each strategy, you probably will apply them in a more complex manner. Sometimes, after testing a first approach, you'll need to go on to a second or even a third, whereas a combination may work best in some situations. To aid your application of these strategies, they appear in an order that we believe parallels the order in which you will usually want to apply them.

Mastering these strategies will benefit you in three ways.

1. Decreasing the number of occasions your anger overwhelms you will soon reduce the strain on your cardiovascular system.

2. Considering your different response options and choosing the most appropriate whenever you are in a stressful situation will reduce the number of occasions you irritate others. By focusing your energies you also will be more likely to get your way.

3. Using strategies that increase your social support and orient you toward affirmations of life should make your life more joyful.

In short, master these strategies, and life will get better!

For some of us, the problem is not our own high level of hostility but that of someone close to us. Chapter 20 focuses upon dealing with someone else's hostility and what you can do to ameliorate your situation.

———

For you or someone you love, this book can be a survival kit stocked with strategies designed to help control hostility. And by mastering these techniques, you may gain control over the rest of your life as well.

Let's get started.

PART I
RECOGNIZING HOSTILITY

"*It always takes Howard a couple of days to relax.*"

CHAPTER 1

Am I at Risk?

"We boil at different degrees."
                    Ralph Waldo Emerson,
                    nineteenth-century U.S. philosopher

"Anger kills. But will it kill *me*?" you ask.

About 20 percent of the general population has levels of hostility high enough to be dangerous to health. Another 20 percent has very low levels, and the rest of the population falls somewhere in between.

Let's determine your profile right now, before you read about the research behind the strong statements in the introduction. At this early juncture, you will be better able to assess your risk without being tempted to second guess how your answers fit with the research findings.

Unfortunately, there is at present no "gold standard" test you can take to gauge whether your hostility level is in the dangerous range. As research over the past decade has pointed more and more to hostility as a health-damaging personality trait, questionnaires, interviews, and other techniques to measure this toxic characteristic have proliferated. But as of now, none of these approaches can be accepted as definitive.

The single questionnaire that appears most valid—in terms of ability to predict increased risk of disease and death in several studies—is the "Hostility" ("Ho" for short) scale, made up of fifty questions from the Minnesota Multiphasic Personality Inventory (MMPI), a widely used psychological test. However, not all studies—for reasons as yet unclear—have found Ho scores to predict health problems. And in a study led by John Barefoot, one of Redford's colleagues at Duke, just twenty-seven of the Ho scale's fifty questions accounted for the prediction of increased death rates

3

in a group of attorneys who were followed up twenty-five years after taking the MMPI while in law school. The other twenty-three questions did not predict this result at all.

It should come as no surprise, therefore, that development of better hostility-assessment tools is an area of intense ongoing research interest. Hence, Redford and his colleagues have grouped, according to their content, the twenty-seven Ho scale questions that did predict higher death rates in the study of lawyers. This led to the formation of three categories of questions that relate to hostile attitudes, emotions, and actions. Using those questions and categories as a starting point, we have added additional questions from other scales and questionnaires, as well as drawn upon our own personal experience (especially Redford's as a typical hostile guy), to develop an expanded set of questions tapping each of these three categories. The result is the new Hostility Questionnaire you are about to take. To make the questionnaire easier to understand and take, we have simplified the format of the questions.

Although this questionnaire is still in the process of being validated in Redford's ongoing research, it should be at least as valid as the Ho scale that is its principal source. We have used it in some of the seminars and workshops we have conducted recently and find that most people taking it feel that it accurately taps their hostility level.

Go ahead now and take the Hostility Questionnaire, which follows. It will provide you with one yardstick by which to measure your hostility level. The last part of this chapter offers a second approach you can use to assess your hostility.

THE HOSTILITY QUESTIONNAIRE

Taking a written test is the first and easiest way to evaluate your hostility level. Your answers, taken all together, should provide a reasonably accurate profile of your attitudes and behaviors, *if* you take care to answer accurately.

It's always tempting to answer such questions as though a parent, fifth-grade teacher, or someone we want to impress were looking over our shoulder! Try to get rid of your chaperone before you begin. Avoid the temptation to choose the response you think you ought to pick, or the one you think would sound right to other people. Answer as spontaneously as you can. Otherwise, you will only be fooling yourself. Unlike the tests you took in school, there are no right or wrong answers here. What *feels* right to you is the correct answer.

Each question describes a specific or general situation that you have probably encountered. If you haven't encountered it, imagine as vividly as you can how you would react in the situation.

After each description you are presented with two responses, A or B, describing how that situation might affect you, or how you might behave under those circumstances. In some instances, neither response may seem to fit, or both may appear equally desirable. This is normal; go ahead and answer anyway, choosing as best you can the single response that is *more likely* for you in that situation.

You may prefer to write down the numbers 1 through 46 on a blank sheet of paper, and then write an "A" or "B" beside each number, to indicate your choice for the corresponding question. This way, others can take the test without being influenced by your responses. In addition, your responses can remain private.

Remember, choose only *one response* for each situation described.

Take as much time as you need to make your choice for each item, but remember that what seems right at first glance—your "gut" reaction—usually represents your true position. On average it should take about fifteen minutes to answer all of the questions.

As you will learn in the next chapter, these may be fifteen minutes that will help you decide you need to make fundamental changes in how you think, feel, and act.

1. A teenager drives by my yard with the car stereo blaring acid rock.

A. I begin to understand why teenagers can't hear.

B. I can feel my blood pressure starting to rise.

2. The person who cuts my hair trims off more than I wanted.

A. I tell him or her what a lousy job he or she did.

B. I figure it'll grow back, and I resolve to give my instructions more forcefully next time.

3. I am in the express checkout line at the supermarket, where a sign reads: "No more than 10 items, please!"

A. I pick up a magazine to pass the time.

B. I glance ahead to see if anyone has more than ten items.

4. Many large cities have a visible number of homeless people.

A. I believe that the homeless are down and out because they lack ambition.

B. The homeless are victims of illness or some other misfortune.

5. There have been times when I was very angry with someone.

A. I was always able to stop short of hitting them.

B. I have, on occasion, hit or shoved them.

6. The newspaper contains a prominent news story about drug-related crime.

A. I wish the government had better educational/drug programs, even for pushers.

B. I wish we could put every drug pusher away for good.

7. The prevalence of AIDS has reached epidemic proportions.

A. This is largely the result of irresponsible behavior on the part of a small proportion of the population.

B. AIDS is a major tragedy.

8. I sometimes argue with a friend or relative.

A. I find profanity an effective tool.

B. I hardly ever use profanity.

9. I am stuck in a traffic jam.

A. I usually am not particularly upset.

B. I quickly start to feel irritated and annoyed.

10. There is a really important job to be done.

    A. I prefer to do it myself.

    B. I am apt to call on my friends or co-workers to help.

11. Sometimes I keep my angry feelings to myself.

    A. Doing so can often prevent me from making a mountain out of a molehill.

    B. Doing so is usually a bad idea.

12. Another driver butts ahead of me in traffic.

    A. I usually flash my lights or honk my horn.

    B. I stay farther back behind such a driver.

13. Someone treats me unfairly.

    A. I usually forget it rather quickly.

    B. I am apt to keep thinking about it for hours.

14. The cars ahead of me on an unfamiliar road start to slow and stop as they approach a curve.

    A. I assume that there is a construction site ahead.

    B. I assume someone ahead had a fender bender.

15. Someone expresses an ignorant belief.

    A. I try to correct him or her.

    B. I am likely to let it pass.

16. I am caught in a slow-moving bank or supermarket line.

    A. I usually start to fume at people who dawdle ahead of me.

    B. I seldom notice the wait.

17. Someone is being rude or annoying.

    A. I am apt to avoid him or her in the future.

    B. I might have to get rough with him or her.

18. An election year rolls around.

   A. I learn anew that politicians are not to be trusted.

   B. I am caught up in the excitement of pulling for my candidate.

19. An elevator stops too long on a floor above where I am waiting.

   A. I soon start to feel irritated and annoyed.

   B. I start planning the rest of my day.

20. I am around someone I don't like.

   A. I try to end the encounter as soon as possible.

   B. I find it hard not to be rude to him or her.

21. I see a very overweight person walking down the street.

   A. I wonder why this person has such little self-control.

   B. I think that he or she might have a metabolic defect or a psychological problem.

22. I am riding as a passenger in the front seat of a car.

   A. I take the opportunity to enjoy the scenery.

   B. I try to stay alert for obstacles ahead.

23. Someone criticizes something I have done.

   A. I feel annoyed.

   B. I try to decide whether the criticism is justified.

24. I am involved in an argument.

   A. I concentrate hard so that I can get my point across.

   B. I can feel my heart pounding, and I breathe harder.

25. A friend or co-worker disagrees with me.

   A. I try to explain my position more clearly.

   B. I am apt to get into an argument with him or her.

26. Someone is speaking very slowly during a conversation.

   A. I am apt to finish his or her sentences.

   B. I am apt to listen until he or she finishes.

27. If they were put on the honor system, most people wouldn't sneak into a movie theater without paying.

   A. That's because they are afraid of being caught.

   B. It's because it would be wrong.

28. I have strong beliefs about rearing children.

   A. I try to reward mine when they behave well.

   B. I make sure that they know what the rules are.

29. I hear news of another terrorist attack.

   A. I feel like lashing out.

   B. I wonder how people can be so cruel.

30. I am talking with my spouse, boyfriend, or girlfriend.

   A. I often find my thoughts racing ahead to what I plan to say next.

   B. I find it easy to pay close attention to what he or she is saying.

31. There have been times in the past when I was really angry.

   A. I have never thrown things or slammed a door.

   B. At times I have thrown something or slammed a door.

32. Life is full of little annoyances.

   A. They often seem to get under my skin.

   B. They seem to roll off my back unnoticed.

33. I disapprove of something a friend has done.

   A. I usually keep such disapproval to myself.

   B. I usually let him or her know about it.

34. I am requesting a seat assignment for an airline flight.

A. I usually request a seat in a specific area of the plane.

B. I generally leave the choice to the agent.

35. I feel a certain way nearly every day of the week.

A. I feel grouchy some of the time.

B. I usually stay on an even keel.

36. Someone bumps into me in a store.

A. I pass it off as an accident.

B. I feel irritated at the person's clumsiness.

37. My spouse, boyfriend, or girlfriend is preparing a meal.

A. I keep an eye out to make sure nothing burns or cooks too long.

B. I either talk about my day or read the paper.

38. A boyfriend or girlfriend calls at the last minute to say that he or she is "too tired to go out tonight," and I am stuck with a pair of fifteen-dollar tickets.

A. I try to find someone else to go with.

B. I tell my friend how inconsiderate he or she is.

39. I recall something that angered me previously.

A. I feel angry all over again.

B. The memory doesn't bother me nearly as much as the actual event did.

40. I see people walking around in shopping malls.

A. Many of them are either shopping or exercising.

B. Many are wasting time.

41. Someone is hogging the conversation at a party.

A. I look for an opportunity to put him or her down.

B. I soon move to another group.

42. At times, I have to work with incompetent people.

    A. I concentrate on my part of the job.

    B. Having to put up with them ticks me off.

43. My spouse, boyfriend, or girlfriend is going to get me a birthday present.

    A. I prefer to pick it out myself.

    B. I prefer to be surprised.

44. I hold a poor opinion of someone.

    A. I keep it to myself.

    B. I let him or her know about it.

45. In most arguments I have, the roles are consistent.

    A. I am the angrier one.

    B. The other person is angrier than I am.

46. Slow-moving lines can often be found in banks and supermarkets.

    A. They are an unavoidable part of modern life.

    B. They are often due to someone's incompetence.

SCORING KEY

CYNICISM	_____
ANGER	_____
AGGRESSION	_____
- -	
TOTAL **HOSTILITY**	_____

Cynicism, anger, and aggression are the three categories we mentioned at the start of this chapter as the ones that accurately measured harmful hostility on the Ho scale. In the next chapter you will learn about these three aspects of hostility that are especially harmful to health:

- *Cynicism:* a mistrusting *attitude* regarding the motives of people in general, leading one to be constantly on guard against the "misbehavior" of others.

- *Anger:* the *emotion* so often engendered by the cynical person's expectation of unacceptable behavior on the part of others.

- *Aggression:* the *behavior* to which many hostile people are driven by the unpleasant negative emotions of anger, irritation, and the like.

The test you just took is designed to reveal where you stand on these three dimensions of hostility that research has shown to predict higher death rates.

To score your Cynicism level, turn back to the test and look at the following items and responses: 3(B), 4(A), 7(A), 10(A), 14(B), 18(A), 21(A), 22(B), 27(A), 30(A), 34(A), 37(A), 40(B), 43(A), and 46(B). Give yourself one point every time your answer agrees with the letter in parentheses after each item number. Thus, if your answers matched the letters in parentheses for eight out of the fifteen Cynicism questions, your Cynicism score would be 8.

These fifteen questions tested the degree to which you believe that people in general are selfish and out mainly for themselves, that you cannot trust them to do the right thing most of the time, and that you are the only one you can really depend on. For example, your having chosen "I glance ahead to see if anyone has more than ten items" instead of "I pick up a magazine to pass the time" when in the express line at the supermarket (item 3), indicates that your level of trust in other people is so low that you expect them to try to sneak through with more than ten items.

Enter your Cynicism score on the appropriate line at the end of the test.

- If your score is 0 to 3, your Cynicism level is very low.

- If your score is 4 to 6, your Cynicism level is probably high enough to be of some concern.

- If your score is 7 or more, your Cynicism level is very high.

To score your Anger level, give yourself one point for each answer that agrees with the letter in parentheses áfter these items: 1(B), 6(B), 9(B), 13(B), 16(A), 19(A), 23(A), 24(B), 29(A), 32(A), 35(A), 36(B), 39(A), 42(B), and 45(A). Enter the total on the line marked "Anger" in the scoring key.

As you probably noticed, these items asked whether you most likely responded with anger, irritation, or annoyance when faced with life's frustrations, such as being stuck in a traffic jam (item 9).

- If your score is 0 to 3, your Anger level is very low.

- If your score is 4 to 6, your Anger level is probably high enough to deserve your attention.

- If your score is 7 or higher, your Anger level is very high.

To score your Aggression level, give yourself one point for each answer that agrees with the letter in parentheses after these items: 2(A), 5(B), 8(A), 11(B), 12(A), 15(A), 17(B), 20(B), 25(B), 26(A), 28(B), 31(B), 33(B), 38(B), 41(A), and 44(B). Write the total on the "Aggression" line of the scoring key.

These items gauge your tendency to express your anger or irritation overtly toward other people, whether physically (e.g., item 5—when angry with someone, "I have, on occasion, hit or shoved them") or verbally (e.g., item 33—when disapproving of something a friend has done, "I usually let him or her know about it").

- If your score is 0 to 3, your Aggression level is very low.

- If your score is 4 to 6, your Aggression level is borderline, and you may want to consider ways to reduce it.

- If your score is 7 or more, you probably need to take serious steps to reduce your Aggression level.

Your Total Hostility score is simply the sum of the three aspects of hostility you have just scored. Add your Cynicism, Anger, and Aggression scores and enter the total on the "Total Hostility" line of the scoring key.

If your Total Hostility score is 10 or less, the research we will review in the next chapter suggests that your hostility level is *below* the range where it is likely to place you at risk of developing health problems. Any score higher than 10 may place you in the group whose hostility level is high enough to increase your risk of health problems.

Your scores on the Cynicism, Anger, and Aggression dimensions of hostility will provide some clues regarding those aspects of your hostility that need changing. For example, if your Cynicism score is 9 but your Anger and Aggression scores are both only 4, this might suggest that you need to focus most on your attitudes toward others.

Before we describe another method of evaluating your hostility, there is one additional way you might wish to use the hostility test just taken, especially if you were unsure of many of your answers or if your scores were borderline or inconclusive. Research in personality assessment has shown that when people who know a person well rate that person on personality tests, the scores are closely related to those obtained by having the person fill out the personality test him- or herself.

If you trust the judgment of someone close to you (a friend or spouse), you might want to ask that person to profile you with the test. Instruct this person to choose the responses to each question as he or she believes *you* would answer. If the score from this person's rating of you agrees closely with yours—within two to three points for the Total Hostility score—then it's likely that your own self-ratings are accurate. If the two scores differ by more than five or six points, and especially if your friend's score is *higher* than yours, you may be underestimating your hostility level.

You can also use the test to rate other people close to you—a spouse, boyfriend, or girlfriend, for instance—to see if their hostility levels may be too high. If so, by lending them this book you might start them toward some helpful "bibliotherapy" of their own!

THE HOSTILITY LOG AND THE
HOSTILITY ROADMAP

A second method of determining your hostility level is to look at your actual day-to-day behavior. Your challenge here is to gather accurate and complete information. Although simply recalling what happened in the course of your day is beneficial, reviewing a written record of your thoughts, feelings, and actions as they occurred provides much more detailed and systematic data.

You can create a Hostility Log by recording at the time or soon afterward throughout your day every aggressive *action* (or urge, e.g., to hit the horn or bang on the elevator door), angry *feeling,* or negative *thought.* Include everything, from thoughts as trivial as "what an asshole that guy is" to mental musings during a meeting in which you imagine your obnoxious supervisor about to ascend the gallows to fully expressed temper tantrums.

As you will recall, *each* of these categories of hostility—cynical attitudes/thoughts, angry emotions/feelings, and aggressive actions/urges—predicted higher death rates in John Barefoot's follow-up study of lawyers. That's why it's important that you be sure to record *each* hostile category in your log.

Whenever you find yourself thinking that someone else is screwing up, being bad, acting inconsiderately, or otherwise behaving inappropriately, enter the incident in your Hostility Log as a *cynical thought.* You may be asking right now, "Well, what if they really *are* being inconsiderate?" Not to worry, the Hostility Roadmap will later address that issue. (By the way, your having that question in your mind, if you did, might suggest that your Cynicism level is in the high range.)

Whenever you find yourself experiencing various negative emotions—ranging from mild pique to annoyance/irritation to anger, all the way up to rage so intense you can barely contain it—describe such feelings in your Hostility Log as an *angry feeling.*

And, finally, whenever you find yourself acting—or even feeling the urge to act—in an aggressive way, enter this as an *aggressive act.* Aggressive acts/urges can range from very mild expressions with your body (frowning at the person ahead of you in line who appears to be taking too long) to moderate actions (honking the horn when in the middle of a traffic jam) to more extreme actions (from shouting angrily at someone to physically assaulting that individual).

Sometimes you may not be able to make an entry when a hostile incident occurs. In such a case, jot down a few notes as soon as feasible and write up your report as soon as you have the necessary privacy. At the end of each day, reexamine your entries to note the quantity and content of incidents. To make your record more thorough and easier to review, we suggest you initially adopt the following format.

HOSTILITY LOG

WHEN: Simply enter date and time.
SCENE: Describe where you are and what is happening.
THOUGHT: List your thoughts.
FEELING: Describe how you feel.
ACTION: Describe what you did.
INVOLVEMENT: How important was this situation to you?

To level with you before we proceed further, we need to reveal that a small percentage of our workshop participants quickly falter in their log keeping. Usually they continue to improve, though diligence usually correlates with progress. If you begin to cheat on log keeping, try to get yourself back on track, but don't quit trying to apply the strategies discussed in upcoming chapters just because you aren't documenting your hostility. Any attempts at hostility control beat none! Still, our main message is that most people can adapt to log keeping, so do give yourself every chance to succeed at this very useful exercise.

To get you started, let's illustrate with the initial entries in the Hostility Log of one Norman Smyth—a composite of a number of patients and research subjects Redford has seen over the years. The actual incidents represent fairly common entries.

FIRST ENTRY

WHEN: 4/27/93, 7:30 A.M.
SCENE: In bed. Clock radio is describing local drug bust involving Colombians.
THOUGHT: Why don't Latin Americans stay in their own countries?
FEELING: Annoyed at Colombian government for not controlling drug production and not rounding up drug distributors.
ACTION: None.
INVOLVEMENT: Low, mainly sleepy.

SECOND ENTRY

WHEN: 4/27/93, 7:49 A.M.
SCENE: At home, checking on kids' rooms. Find clothes on floor.
THOUGHT: Darn kids, why can't they pick up clothes?!
FEELING: Irritation. Also felt tense and wired.
ACTION: Yelled at Suzy.
INVOLVEMENT: Very upset.

THIRD ENTRY

WHEN: 4/27/93, 8:15 A.M.
SCENE: Beltway. Radio reports trade deficit with Japan.
THOUGHT: Japs take too much and give too little.
FEELING: Mildly irritated.
ACTION: None.
INVOLVEMENT: Mild.

FOURTH ENTRY

WHEN: 4/27/93, 8:22 A.M.
SCENE: Beltway. Another car speeds past and cuts in ahead to exit. I have to hit brakes.
THOUGHT: The nerve of some people!
FEELING: Rage at first, then still annoyed for several minutes.
ACTION: Blasted horn for 5 sec.
INVOLVEMENT: High. Nuts like that jackass cause accidents!

Obviously, the two entries pertaining to occurrences on the beltway were made after the fact, perhaps while waiting in traffic for a light to change or after arriving at the office.

FIFTH ENTRY

WHEN: 4/27/93, 9:30 A.M.
SCENE: Tuesday marketing meeting. Bob Schwartz pushing his plan.
THOUGHT: Bob Schwartz is a brown-noser and a jerk.
FEELING: Pissed off at Bob.
ACTION: None. Just sat and fumed.
INVOLVEMENT: High.

No additional entries exist until several recorded that evening. One of these late entries described an incident that occurred while Norman was on the beltway driving home. Another involved a major blowup with his wife, and the last entry for 4/27/93 was set in a shopping center near Norman's home.

Late that evening, Norman looked at his notebook. He first noted that eight entries put him in the group at high risk for developing cardiovascular disease. He also noted that he had yelled at his daughter and wife as well as blasted his horn on the beltway, three acts of aggression that again put him at risk.

With the help of a second aid, a Hostility Roadmap (figure 1.1), Norman subjected his Log to further scrutiny. At the top of the Roadmap is a blank space, where Norman could write in, or simply focus in turn upon, each entry in his Log. After carefully reviewing his first Log entry, Norman asked himself the first question on the Roadmap. "Was that radio report important enough to be worth my continued attention?" For his first entry, he concluded it was, because Jimmy and Suzy would soon be old enough to be exposed to drugs.

Still following the Hostility Roadmap, Norman next asked whether his action/feeling/thought was justified. For his first entry, he concluded that he was justified in being angry at Colombian officials because of the damage drugs were causing. But maybe he couldn't really blame everyone from that country, so he wasn't justified in disliking everyone who lived there. After all, he had never met these people and actually didn't even know how much control they had over the drug traffic.

Norman's last question concerned whether he had an effective response. He concluded he couldn't influence Colombian officials, but might influence his own representatives. He decided to write a note to his senators and congressional representative, urging legis-

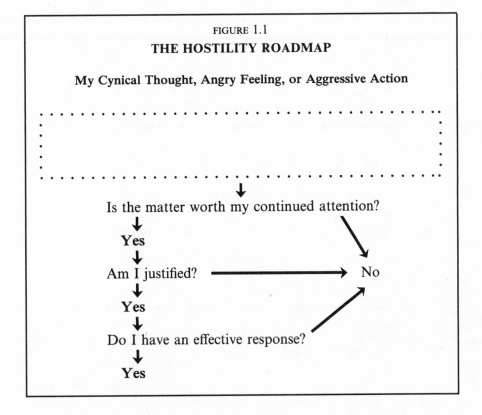

FIGURE 1.1

THE HOSTILITY ROADMAP

My Cynical Thought, Angry Feeling, or Aggressive Action

lation to strengthen drug patrols. He made a note to that effect below the entry in his Log.

Norman subjected in turn each entry to the three questions on the Roadmap. Every time he got a no, he stopped and made note of the inappropriateness of his hostile thought, feeling, or action. If he answered yes, he went on to the next question. All of this went very quickly, once he got the hang of it.

When Norman asked the question about the importance of the matter, he dropped one entry. Too bad he'd lost his temper with Suzy over the clothes left on the floor—the matter was so trivial. (Mainly he wanted to build bridges between himself and his daughter.)

When Norman asked his justification question for his other entries, he gave up his anger against the Japanese, but stayed upset at the inconsiderate driver. He wasn't sure about Bob Schwartz. Maybe the problem was Bob. But Bob had never actually mistreated Norman. Or anyone else—at least, that Norman had ever observed. But Bob is a brown-noser, Norman decided. Norman resolved to stay vigilant but not to let Bob upset him so much.

"Do I have an effective response?" made another entry fall by the way. The inconsiderate driver deserved to be taken down a peg or two but, unfortunately, blasting his horn had mainly irritated only Norman and other nearby drivers on the beltway.

Norman was left with the letter he planned to write, his resolve to pay closer attention to Bob, and the realization that yelling at Suzy and his wife over trivial matters accomplished little but to alienate them.

After using the Roadmap to evaluate each of his Log entries that evening, Norman concluded that most of his cynical thoughts, angry feelings, and aggressive actions that day had been:

- not really worth the attention he'd devoted to them;

- not really justified by the circumstances;

- not worth pursuing, as he had no effective response available.

And where there was effective action to be taken, he took it.

After a week of keeping his Log each day and subjecting the entries to the Roadmap each evening, Norman concluded that he did have too much hostility. Maybe his high score on the Hostility Questionnaire wasn't as far off the mark as he had thought when he scored it.

Start right away keeping your own Hostility Log. First acquire a notebook. Choose a sturdy one, small enough to fit into your pocket. In the front of your notebook, write down the format Norman used—When, Scene, and so on—for reference when you make each entry. (Substitute a different structure if you prefer. The important point is to record your hostile thoughts, feelings, and actions.)

Carry your little notebook around with you constantly for one week. Every time you act aggressively, feel angry, or have a cynical mistrusting thought, jot down notes as soon as you can.

At the end of each day, count the number of entries in your Log. If you have more than two or three entries a day, you probably are part of the 20 percent of people whose high hostility may possibly harm them over time.

Another test is to evaluate what percentage of your entries

were occasions in which the matter wasn't worth the attention you gave it, your feelings were not justified, or you got upset despite having no effective response. If more than 25 percent of your entries got a Roadmap no on any of these three questions, this is another indication that you are probably too hostile. That is, if more than a quarter of your hostile thoughts, feelings, or actions are not worth the attention you gave them, were not justified, or were experienced despite your having no effective response, then you are probably having too many of them.

In addition to their initial value as diagnostic tools, keeping a Hostility Log and using the Hostility Roadmap to evaluate your entries will have numerous other benefits.

- Taking formal notes encourages careful observations of actual behaviors, feelings, and thoughts while or soon after they occur. Engaging in these kinds of observations will make you more self-aware and objective.

- Having this written record allows you to review what triggered your reaction systematically and rationally and to examine how you actually behaved. Given this information, you can think about what your other behavioral options were and evaluate how well you handled the situation. If some other behaviors you will learn about later in this book would have been more effective options, you can make a mental note to try to react in the preferred manner whenever a similar situation arises.

- Once a Log entry is made, you have a permanent record. You can reexamine old situations on as many different occasions and from as many different perspectives as you deem useful.

Now that you have gained a better sense of your hostility level, you know whether your health is at increased risk because of hostility. If your hostility is in the dangerous range, read on for the evidence that hostility does indeed damage health. You will also learn how hostility wreaks its harm, as well as something about encouraging research showing that behavioral techniques to reduce and counter the harmful effects of hostility appear to prolong life.

We shall also take a look into the future, as we review new research that provides clues about the neurobiological basis of hostility and its health-harming effects—clues that may point by the twenty-first century to a real "magic bullet" to counter the harmful effects of hostility.

PART II
THE SCIENTIFIC BACKGROUND

Clinic for the Study of Aggressive Behavior cartoon by John Chase.

CHAPTER **2**

The Facts About Hostility

"Nice guys finish last."

Leo Durocher,
twentieth-century U.S. baseball manager

Courtesy of Sandy Dean

AN EVOLUTIONARY TALE:
MARTIN MEETS ENEMIES
ON THE OPEN ROAD

Martin had at least three reasons to feel satisfied as he pulled out of the parking lot. The air conditioner in the company car was already making a dent in the eastern North Carolina July heat that had built up while he was making his sales rounds in the county hospital. The ten automatic blood-pressure monitors he had persuaded the operating room supervisor to order put him over his quota for the quarter—the bonus would come in handy when Betty took the boys to buy their school clothes. And with a little luck he'd make the Raleigh beltway before rush hour, getting home in time for dinner with his family.

Martin's good mood lasted until he was accelerating through the last outskirts of town. He loathed the prospect of the two-lane blacktop, which stretched for forty miles ahead until it widened to four lanes east of Raleigh. "Those damned slowpokes are sure to be out there making it hell for the rest of us!" Martin thought.

He mashed the gas pedal and enjoyed the surge of the V-8 quickly bringing the speed up to his usual six to seven miles above the fifty-five-miles-per-hour speed limit. All was fine for the first ten to fifteen miles, but then up ahead loomed a large, slow-moving truck laden with pulpwood, an all-too-common road hazard in this part of the state.

"At least there's only one car behind that damned truck now—if he'll go ahead and pass," Martin mused, "I can scoot by and not get stuck in another convoy."

But the other car—an older sedan, much in need of washing—didn't pull out, even though Martin could see a clear road ahead of the truck. "Asshole!" Martin barked toward the driver in the sedan. "*Move* it while there's room!"

As Martin drew closer, the sedan continued to sit there behind the truck, apparently happy to dawdle along at fifty-three miles per hour. Martin flashed his lights several times, exhorting the other driver, "C'mon, dummy, pass *now!*"

Unable to stand the delay any longer, Martin eased to the left, saw open road ahead, and pulled out at full power to pass *both* the slow-moving car and the truck. Even before he made it past the sedan, he realized his mistake—a rapidly approaching oncoming car had rounded the curve ahead. Quickly turning on his right turn signal, Martin looked to pull back in behind the pulpwood truck.

But the fellow in the car to his right wasn't slowing down to let him back in! In fact, he actually speeded up so that Martin had to slam on his brakes and drop back. He barely maneuvered back into the right-hand lane before the oncoming car streaked past, lights flashing and horn blasting.

"Dumb bastard!" Martin raged. "Too chicken to pass the truck himself, but not considerate enough to let me back in when I try to pass!"

Even though he'd been able to keep his promise to Betty to lay off cigarettes this whole trip, Martin found himself rummaging through the glove compartment and pulling out the reserve pack he kept hidden there. As he pulled the smoke into his lungs his rage began to subside, but not completely. He was tempted to take down the license number of the slow-moving car and turn it in with a complaint for reckless driving.

As these thoughts percolated through Martin's mind—somewhere in his left cerebral cortex—they sent out a wake-up call to a group of hypothalamic nerve cells deeper within his brain. These cells in turn sent messages to a way station even farther down in the base of his brain, where they caused outgoing nerves to signal the adrenal glands sitting atop each of Martin's kidneys to pump large doses of both adrenaline and cortisol into his bloodstream.

"Murderer!" Martin seethed. "At least *potential* murderer, that's what that driver was."

As the adrenaline reached Martin's heart it began to pound harder and faster. If his blood pressure registered this high in his doctor's office, he'd be on blood-pressure pills.

"That bastard belongs in jail!"

At the same time, the activated hypothalamic emergency center stimulated sympathetic nerves to constrict the arteries carrying blood to Martin's skin, kidneys, and intestines, while the adrenaline was causing the arteries to his muscles to open up wide.

All of these biological changes Martin experienced on the two-lane highway would have been very useful if he, like his ancestors of more than two million years ago, were being attacked by a sabre-toothed tiger. A person in danger of being slashed by tooth or claw has no need to worry about digesting a meal or wasting precious body fluids on urine formation. It's also better to keep the blood away from the skin on the body surface. But pump that blood in buckets to those muscles that are so essential for "fight or flight"!

The extra cortisol now in Martin's bloodstream prolonged and amplified the adrenaline effects on his heart and arteries—very useful, too, if one is running away from a sabre-toothed tiger or trying to keep another male in your hunter-gatherer group from stealing your mate.

Meanwhile, the fired-up cells back in his hypothalamus were shutting off Martin's parasympathetic nervous system so that the blood-pressure rise and other adrenaline effects were not quickly terminated by the parasympathetic "calming response" but continued to keep his circulatory system churning away.

The adrenaline and cortisol also caused his immune system to go into a holding pattern—again, not a bad idea in situations where serious bodily harm is a real possibility. If you're slashed and bleeding, you don't want your immune system to start making antibodies to your own tissues.

As the angry thoughts and feelings continued, Martin's heart also continued to pump out blood far in excess of the needs of his body, which was simply sitting there in the car heading back toward Raleigh. Indeed, Martin's body sent messages back up to his brain about the bodily effects—pounding heart; sweaty palms; deep, rapid breathing—of the massive adrenaline surge. These messages reinforced his perception that real danger must be close at hand.

Martin's blood pressure rose quickly, and, somewhere on the smooth inner lining of one of the coronary arteries that supply blood to his heart muscle, a patch of endothelial cells was eroded by the rapidly swirling currents of blood rushing past—much like a river bank when the stream is at flood.

To make matters worse, Martin's platelets—tiny subcellular clotting elements circulating in the blood—hurried to the damaged spot of the artery. Two million years ago this would have been normal and useful, for if the artery had been slashed by that sabre-toothed tiger, the platelets sticking to the spot would seal the hole and stop the bleeding.

Only there was no tiger, and the artery wasn't slashed. Nevertheless, just as it has in humans since time immemorial, the adrenaline stimulated more of Martin's platelets to clump at the scratched arterial surface, where they released some chemicals that stimulated the muscle cells in the artery wall to migrate to the inner surface, where they would grow and multiply. Other blood cells called macrophages were summoned to the scene to gobble up the injured tissue and debris.

The adrenaline also stimulated Martin's fat cells to empty their contents into his bloodstream—to provide energy for the effort he would need to exert had a real emergency occurred. Because he really wasn't burning up this fat in order to escape from the tiger or fight a rival trying to steal his mate—but just sitting there fuming in his car—Martin's liver converted the fat into cholesterol. This excess cholesterol was absorbed into the clump of platelets and macrophages on the scratched artery, and some of it even made its way into the artery wall.

Let's look for a moment into Martin's future. We see many more such arousals of his fight-or-flight response, many of them stimulated by nothing more than his own cynical expectations that others will be mean and selfish, rather than by what they actually do. Each time this happens, the scratched spot inside his coronary artery will be damaged anew. And each time, the cholesterol formed from the unused fat that pours into his bloodstream will accumulate in the macrophages and smooth muscle cells that have been drawn to the spot.

For reasons still not fully understood, these cholesterol-filled "foam cells" don't clear out but just sit there. Over the course of a few more years, they mature into an arteriosclerotic plaque that nearly blocks off the flow of blood into that coronary artery entirely. A day will come when this plaque is traumatized again, perhaps one morning when the traffic on the way to work really annoys Martin. The platelet plug formed this time will be so big that it completely closes off the remaining small opening in the artery. A clot will form, and the life-sustaining blood will no longer be able to pass through to nourish Martin's heart muscle. The blood-starved heart muscle downstream will be injured as a result; a portion will die. When this happens, Martin will have become one of the 500,000-plus Americans who have heart attacks each year.

But all this is several years off. Let us return now to the present, where we note that Martin does arrive safely at his home in a Raleigh suburb—actually, no more than fifteen minutes later than would have been the case if he had succeeded in passing the slow-moving car and the pulpwood truck. As he comes through the door he yells at one of the boys for having left a bicycle in the drive. Betty decides to overlook the smell of cigarettes on his breath—better to remind him later of his promise to quit.

Instead of sitting with Betty to share the good news about his sales, Martin pours himself a double scotch. It's gone in under five minutes, and he pours another. Feeling somewhat calmer, he has two extra servings of lasagna for dinner. Somehow, this helps him feel better. About 11:00 that night, still feeling restless, he raids the freezer for a big serving of ice cream. Finally he crawls into bed beside Betty, who fell asleep two hours before. After another half-hour of tossing, Martin drifts off into a fitful sleep.

The story you have just read is based on the findings of more than two decades of scientific research on the role of stress in medical disease. All of the thoughts, feelings, actions, bodily changes, and other "risky" behaviors—smoking, drinking, and eating too much—we describe in Martin have been found among people who suffer from the Hostility Syndrome, a group of characteristics that places many people at higher risk of developing severe, life-threatening illness. Redford has been closely involved in this research on hostility and health. Therefore, in the rest of this chapter he will tell you about this research, as it has been conducted with his colleagues in laboratories at Duke as well as at other research centers around the country.

If you prefer to skip the account of the scientific work, you can turn directly to the summary of these findings on page 60.

IN THE BEGINNING
THERE WAS TYPE A

When I entered Harvard College in the fall of 1959 I took Dr. George Goethals's freshman seminar, "The Behavioral Sciences." Our first assignment was to write a paper on "The mind–body problem." After thirty-three years of college, medical school, internship, and residency in internal medicine, research training at the National Institute of Mental Health (NIMH), and as a faculty member at Duke, I am still working on that assignment.

When I took up my faculty position at Duke—in the Department of Psychiatry's Division of Psychosomatic Medicine—in the summer of 1972, the hottest research topic in psychosomatic medicine was Type A behavior and its relation to coronary heart disease. First described by Meyer Friedman and Ray Rosenman, two San Francisco cardiologists, Type A behavior consisted of several psychological characteristics—always being in a hurry, easily moved to hostility and anger, and high levels of competitiveness and ambition—that they observed far more often in their patients with coronary heart disease than in patients with other types of illness.

Based on this observed *association* between Type A behavior and coronary disease in their patients, Friedman and Rosenman obtained a grant from the National Heart, Lung and Blood Institute (NHLBI) to do a prospective (forward-looking) study of more than three thousand healthy men to see if those who are Type A subsequently developed more coronary disease than men without Type A characteristics (called Type B by Friedman and Rosenman). This study, known as the Western Collaborative Group Study (WCGS), found that over an eight-and-a-half year follow-up period, twice as many of the Type A men developed coronary disease as did the Type B men. This increased coronary risk among the Type A men was not accounted for by the traditional risk factors; *something* besides smoking, cholesterol, and high blood pressure was responsible for their higher coronary rates.

It's important to appreciate the magnitude of Friedman and Rosenman's accomplishment in the WCGS. Everyone "knows" that stress is bad for the heart. Even two thousand years ago it is recorded in the Bible (Acts, chapter 5) that Ananias and his wife Sapphira dropped dead on the spot (presumably from stress-induced cardiac arrest) when they were severely chastised by Peter for holding back some of the proceeds from a land sale after apparently giving him and the Disciples all the proceeds to help their work.

Despite such folk wisdom and a considerable amount of research in psychosomatic medicine during the first half of the twentieth century, it was not until Friedman and Rosenman's demonstration of increased coronary risk among Type A men in the WCGS that any psychological trait had been shown to *predict* any disease in a prospective study. The famous Framingham Study had proven that high cholesterol, smoking, and high blood pressure are risk factors for coronary disease by showing that healthy persons who had these risk factors were more likely to develop heart disease. Similarly, the WCGS had now shown that a psychological trait—Type A behavior—predicted coronary disease. Publication of the WCGS findings during the early 1970s elevated the scientific respectability of psychosomatic medicine to a level higher than ever before.

It also attracted the interest of a great many young researchers, including me. During my medical school and NIMH days, I had focused my research on the role of stress as a causal factor in high blood pressure, or hypertension. It had been easy to show that when they were stressed in the lab, hypertensive patients showed larger blood-pressure increases than patients with other illnesses. But this really didn't help prove that such larger stress responses caused the high blood pressure, because the patients' bigger responses could simply be an *effect* of their having the disease.

Type A behavior, on the other hand, had passed the critical test used by epidemiologists to identify potential causal agents for any disease: Its presence *prior* to the appearance of the disease had *predicted* who would go on to develop the disease—in this case America's number-one killer, coronary heart disease.

When I joined the Duke faculty, Ewald Busse, the chairman of the Psychiatry Department, asked about new areas (besides hypertension) into which I would like to expand my research focus. I enthusiastically told him about my growing interest in Type A behavior. Dr. Busse asked if I knew who was doing the best research in this area. When I told him about Friedman and Rosenman's WCGS, he quickly made the kind of decision that seems to come so easily to really good leaders: He said, "Well, I guess we need to get one of them to come to Duke and help you get started."

When I called Ray Rosenman to tell him of my interest in doing research on Type A behavior and asked if he could visit Duke to discuss the possibilities, he responded immediately in the affirmative. His visit confirmed my conviction to make Type A my major research focus, and shortly thereafter, with support from an NIMH grant, I went to San Francisco to get instruction from Friedman and Rosenman in their structured interview technique—then, as now, the "gold standard"—for assessing Type A behavior.

I learned that to assess Type A behavior one cannot simply attend to *what* a person says; it is more important to be attuned to *how* he or she is saying it. For example, if you ask, "Do you rush and hurry in most things?" and the person being interviewed pauses for what seems an eternity and then finally answers—in slow and measured tones—"Why . . . yes . . . I probably do . . . rush . . . most of the . . . time," the content of the answer is Type A (yes to rushing and hurrying), but the slow and measured pace and tone of the answer are definitely Type B.

On the other hand, if the person being interviewed responds to the same question about rushing and hurrying in a rapid, staccato voice—"Not me, boy. Oh, no, I always take life slow and easy, you bet!"—the content may be Type B, but the tone is surely Type A. It takes training and experience to be an accurate assessor of Type A behavior, but once one has mastered the method, it is possible to make reliable ratings, in much the same way it takes time and training for a cardiologist to be able to interpret electrocardiograms.

Upon my return to Duke, all that remained was to decide where and how to start my Type A research. When they performed autopsies on men who died in the WCGS, Friedman and Rosenman had found that the men they had categorized originally as Type A had more extensive arteriosclerotic blockages in their coronary arteries than the Type B men. Why not see, I asked, if we find more coronary arteriosclerosis among *living* Type A patients?

At this time, the Duke cardiologists were weekly doing several coronary angiograms—an X-ray study in which a small tube is threaded up an artery to the heart, where it is used to inject a dye and thereby make visual the coronary arteries that feed the heart muscle. It would be a simple matter, therefore, to do the Type A interview on patients getting the angiograms and see if the Type A patients had more arteriosclerotic blockages.

The opportunity to get this study started came sooner than anticipated, in the form of a psychology graduate student, Jim Blumenthal, who wanted to do his Ph.D. thesis in the psychosomatic area. Jim quickly mastered the use of Friedman and Rosenman's structured interview to assess Type A behavior and was soon off to the cardiology wards doing Type A interviews on 142 patients scheduled for coronary angiography.

His findings served only to strengthen my confidence that Type A behavior contributes to the development of coronary heart disease: Among those patients with minimal blockages on their angiogram, Jim found that equal proportions were Type A and B; among those with moderately severe blockages, more than over 70 percent were Type A; and among those with very severe blockages—at least two coronary arteries totally blocked off by arteriosclerotic plaques—more than *90 percent* were Type A.

By the time Jim's paper was published in the prestigious cardiology journal *Circulation,* at least two other research groups—one at Columbia and one at Boston University—had also found more severe coronary arteriosclerosis among patients undergoing coronary angiography.

All the research findings pointed to the conclusion that, like high cholesterol, high blood pressure, and smoking, Type A behavior is a real coronary disease risk factor. Indeed, this was exactly the conclusion reached by a blue-ribbon panel convened in 1978 by the NHLBI to evaluate all the research on Type A behavior and coronary disease.

Before the ink was dry on the blue-ribbon panel's report, however, new studies began to cast doubt on the Type A hypothesis. Several studies of patients undergoing coronary angiography, for example, failed to confirm Jim's observation of more severe blockages in the Type A patients.

My first inclination was to look for flaws in these negative studies. Several had used questionnaires, rather than the "gold standard" structured interview, to assess Type A behavior and could be dismissed on that ground. Others examined very small numbers of patients and, therefore, lacked adequate "statistical power" to detect a real Type A–arteriosclerosis relationship, even if it were present. For a while, it was possible for the Type A adherents to reject these negative studies as flawed and therefore not worthy of our concern.

As time went on, however, I began to have my own doubts that Type A was the best we could do in defining the personality profile that causes coronary disease. These doubts were fueled by three observations.

The first grew out of some research I had been doing. From 1975 through 1980 we had been doing Type A interviews and collecting other psychological data (including the Minnesota Multiphasic Personality Inventory, or MMPI) on nearly all patients undergoing coronary angiography at Duke. When we examined the relationship between this "gold standard" Type A measure and coronary arteriosclerosis in a very large sample of nearly 2,300 patients, we found that Type A *was* significantly associated with increased arteriosclerosis, but only weakly so and only among the younger patients. There was clearly a relationship between Type A and coronary disease here, but it was not nearly as strong as I had expected.

The second observation that shook my confidence in the Type A hypothesis came from a study done by Dr. Richard Shekelle and his colleagues, which followed up more than three thousand initially healthy men who had multiple coronary risk factors and who had been assessed as Type A or B through the use of the structured interview. After more than seven years of follow-up, there was absolutely no increase in coronary events among the Type A men. This study, the Multiple Risk Factor Intervention Trial (MRFIT), had used the "gold standard" interview assessment, had followed as large a sample of men as the WCGS, *and* still failed to confirm any increased coronary risk among the Type A men.

The third observation that forced me to rethink my position was one suggesting that not all but only some aspects of Type A behavior are bad for the heart. In his original study, in addition to the Type A interview, Jim Blumenthal had seen a need to obtain a measure of hostility as an aspect of Type A behavior that might be especially harmful. Jim asked his other adviser at Duke, Larry Thompson, a psychologist, to suggest a measure of hostility he might get from the patients in addition to the Type A interview.

Larry suggested a couple of hostility questionnaires that Jim might use but told him that he already had mimeographed copies of one—the Cook and Medley "Ho" scale, made up of fifty questions from the MMPI—that Jim could take and use if he wished. Following the path of least resistance, Jim administered the Ho questionnaire to the patients in his study. Although we never published the findings from these Ho questionnaires—probably because we were so caught up in publishing the Type A results at the time—we did note a positive association between higher Ho scores and more severe arteriosclerosis.

I remembered this earlier observation as I pondered what to make of all the negative Type A studies. Since by this time we had administered the MMPI to 424 of our patients undergoing angiography, it was possible to reexamine the fifty Ho scale questions and see if higher Ho counts correlated with more severe arteriosclerosis. The results were clear: Not only did people with higher Ho counts have more severe arteriosclerosis, but the Ho scores also were associated with arteriosclerosis even more strongly than were Type A scores.

Yes, in the beginning there was Type A. But now it was time to narrow the focus of my research and concentrate on hostility as a more likely candidate for a health-damaging personality trait.

THE HOSTILITY STORY: THANK GOODNESS GRANT DAHLSTROM IS A PACKRAT!

Serendipity is defined as the making of pleasant discoveries by accident. In one respect, Jim Blumenthal's choice of the Ho scale to assess hostility in his Ph.D. research was an accident, depending as it did upon Larry Thompson's possession of a ready-to-use stack of Ho questionnaires. Very soon after we published our paper showing increased arteriosclerosis among patients with higher Ho scores, there began to appear portents of "pleasant discoveries."

The first was a letter from Dr. Richard Shekelle asking how to score the MMPI for the Ho scale. He had collected MMPI data on a sample of more than 1,800 middle-aged men working at a Western Electric factory in Chicago in the late 1950s and now wanted to see if their Ho scores predicted health problems over the ensuing twenty-year period. The second portent came in the form of a telephone call from Dr. John Barefoot, a psychologist who was doing a follow-up study of 255 doctors who had taken the MMPI while in medical school at the University of North Carolina (UNC), also in the late 1950s. John was working with Grant Dahlstrom, a UNC psychology professor, who was one of the original developers of the MMPI. Dahlstrom had been administering the MMPI to various student groups at UNC for decades and had saved every one. Like Dr. Shekelle, John Barefoot had been stimulated by our paper to see whether Ho scores predicted health outcomes.

In both cases the Ho score predicted serious health problems over the twenty to twenty-five years after the Western Electric men and the UNC doctors had taken the MMPI. As they aged from twenty-five to fifty, those UNC doctors whose Ho scores had been in the upper half at age twenty-five were four to five times more likely than those with lower scores to develop coronary disease and nearly seven times more likely to die from any cause. Similarly, those Western Electric men with higher Ho scores were one-and-a-half times more likely to develop coronary disease or die from any cause than those with lower scores.

While very reliable statistically, the impact of high Ho scores on death rates was smaller in the Western Electric men. We attributed this smaller effect to the older age of the Western Electric men at the time they started the study—forty-five on average. In the study of UNC doctors, most of those who died before age fifty were already dead by age forty-five. A study like the Western Electric Study that considered people starting at age forty-five would be missing all those doctors with high Ho scores who had already died. Those who survived to age forty-five were probably more resistant to the health-damaging effects of hostility, which would explain the smaller impact of high Ho scores in the middle-aged Western Electric men.

This weakening impact of hostility on health with increasing age is consistent with other risk factors, such as smoking and high cholesterol, which also become weaker predictors of health problems as age increases.

Another interesting finding in the Western Electric Study was a discovery of increased *cancer* deaths among the men with high Ho scores that just missed the ".05" level of statistical significance required in science for a result to be considered "real." This suggested that in addition to contributing to higher death rates via increased coronary rates, hostility might also be contributing to increased risk of cancer as well.

Dahlstrom's "packrat" tendency to save all the old MMPIs in his possession has paid other dividends over the years. Incoming UNC students during the mid-1960s were required to take the MMPI at registration. The seven thousand MMPIs Dahlstrom saved from those years have enabled Dr. Ilene Siegler of our Duke Behavioral Medicine research group to start the UNC Alumni Heart Study, which I shall describe later in this chapter.

Dr. Dahlstrom also saved the MMPIs that were given to a group of 118 UNC law students in the 1950s. When John Barefoot followed them up recently, he found that among those lawyers whose Ho scores had been in the highest quarter of their class twenty-five years earlier, nearly 20 percent were dead by age fifty; in contrast, only 4 percent of those with Ho scores in the lowest quarter had died.

It was in this study of lawyers that we identified questions from the Ho scale reflecting *cynical mistrust* of others, the frequent experience of *angry feelings,* and the overt expression of this cynicism and anger in *aggressive behavior* as the only questions that were actually accounting for the overall Ho score's prediction of higher mortality rates. These questions and others reflecting these three aspects of hostility are the ones we have adapted for the Hostility Questionnaire you took in chapter 1.

To see how these aspects of hostility color our everyday life, let us return to the story of Martin that began this chapter. First, even though he had ample reason to be in a pleasant mood as he left the hospital, when he hit the highway his *cynical mistrust* led to concerns that quickly placed him on guard against the "incompetent" drivers he presumed he would find ahead. When he noticed a driver apparently fulfilling his pessimistic expectations by not passing a slow-moving truck, Martin quickly became *angry* and actually expressed his ire by the *aggressive behavior* of flashing his lights at the "cautious" driver.

There have also been studies that failed to find that hostility predicts health problems. In one, a follow-up study of Medical College of Georgia (MCG) graduates similar to John Barefoot's UNC doctors study, Dr. Edward McCranie and his colleagues found that Ho scores obtained when the doctors had been visiting MCG for their admission interviews did not predict subsequent health problems. Reviewers of the study spotted a clue as to why this study found no prediction of health problems by Ho scores: Because they wanted to appear in the best light for possible medical school admission, the applicants likely answered the Ho scale questions in a more socially desirable—that is, less hostile—way than they would have if so much had not been riding (potentially) on their answers. The very low Ho scores—average of 9 versus 16 in the UNC doctors—confirmed this suspicion.

Gloria Leon, a Minnesota psychologist, and her colleagues reported another study in which Ho scores failed to predict health outcomes in about 250 Minnesota businessmen who had taken the MMPI when their average age was between forty-five and fifty. The MMPIs in this study were not tainted by the testing situation, as had been the case for the MCG doctors study. The failure of Ho scores to predict health problems in this study might have resulted from the small sample size and older age of the men.

A third negative study reported by Dr. Marcia Davis and her colleagues followed up more than one thousand University of Minnesota graduates who had completed the MMPI as undergraduates during the 1950s. This study did not suffer from test-situation problems and used younger subjects on whom the Ho effect would be expected to be larger than in middle-aged folks. Therefore, we must acknowledge her negative findings.

Taken altogether, most of the studies using the Ho scale make a strong case that hostility is a true health-damaging personality trait. However, because some studies found no correlation between Ho scores and health problems, this suggests that the Ho scale is probably not a definitive measure of hostility. This impression grows stronger when we recall that in John Barefoot's follow-up study of UNC lawyers only about half of the Ho questions were predictive of higher death rates.

Nevertheless, the Ho scale does appear to be tapping into a personality trait that places some people at higher risk of health problems. And as we shall learn later in this chapter, high Ho scores do correlate with biological characteristics and health behaviors that certainly have the potential to damage health.

Besides the Ho scale, other studies have used different questionnaires to measure hostility or cynicism and found these measures to correlate with the development of coronary arteriosclerosis and to predict increased risk of death from heart disease and other causes. For example, using only a three-question hostility scale, investigators in Finland found that persons who had higher scores had a more than fourfold higher death rate during a follow-up period than those with lower scores.

My confidence in the harmful health effects of hostility is reinforced by results from other studies that used Friedman and Rosenman's Type A structured interview to assess hostility. Earlier I described how the tone of the answer rather than the overt content tells us whether someone rushes and hurries. The same is true for hostility. Here's an example. You ask the person being interviewed, "When you get angry, do you show it?" If the response is, "Of course not! What do you take me for?" the content is not hostile—the person does not express anger—but the tone and challenge to the interviewer is dripping with contempt. Chalk this person up as hostile.

Conversely, if the answer—this time in a calm, slow voice—is, "Oh, I suppose . . . if I were angry . . . it would probably show," the content is hostile, but the tone is not. A person answering this way belongs in the low-hostility group.

Because the interviews in the earlier Type A studies were tape recorded, it has now been possible for researchers to reanalyze those tapes, scoring them as I have described not only for the overall Type A score but also for the "rush/hurry" and hostility components. When this was done for both Friedman and Rosenman's original subjects in the WCGS and for the men in the MRFIT study, the "rush/hurry" score did not predict heart attacks; in contrast, the hostility score was a strong predictor, even when the standard risk factors were taken into account.

Does hostility predict health troubles for women as well as men? Most of the epidemiologic research relating hostility to health troubles has focused on men. Women are more difficult to study because fewer of them develop heart disease as early in life as men. Nevertheless, what information there is available on hostility in women does confirm a similar pattern. Hostile women do have more severe coronary arteriosclerosis and higher death rates when followed up over periods of several years.

Although the studies using interview assessments of hostility have more consistently found hostility-predicting health problems than studies using questionnaire measures, the interview technique requires considerable training before an investigator can use it reliably. Questionnaires, on the other hand, are far easier to use, especially in large-scale epidemiologic studies. Large groups of people must be followed to find enough developing heart disease and other health problems to detect real but possibly small adverse effects of a trait like hostility.

People like John Barefoot at Duke, Paul Costa at the National Institute on Aging, Tim Smith at the University of Utah, and Aron Seigman at the University of Maryland are hard at work trying to develop more reliable and valid ways of measuring hostility and its various components.

I am confident that eventually they will be successful. In the meanwhile, I am also confident that the available evidence using a wide range of measures does make a very strong case that hostility is a personality trait that exerts most deleterious effects on physical health.

———

I want also to note the harmful psychological effects of hostility. As a group, hostile people are unhappy. Timothy Smith, a University of Utah researcher, and his colleagues have found that college students who score high on the Ho scale report more hassles and negative life events, along with less social support.

Married life also has problems for hostile people. Smith reports that during discussion of a topic on which they disagree, married couples with one or both members scoring high on the Ho scale exhibited more instances of dominating, acrimonious interchanges than couples with both members scoring low on the Ho scale. In another study, Smith and his colleagues report that individuals with high levels of hostility report less marital satisfaction and more marital conflict. (This was more true for men than for women.)

Similar results are reported by David Mace, a marriage therapist (who with his wife, Vera, founded ACME, Associated Couples for Marital Enrichment). He calls management of anger the "one key issue that would explain why so many marriages, embarked upon with such high hopes, finally falter and fail." In the Maces' view, failure to deal effectively with anger destroys intimacy by resulting in too many or too few disagreements.

Arguments between spouses can become bitter because the individuals know each other well enough to attack in ways that hurt the most. Each partner feels frustrated, hurt, and even angrier. Arguments escalate, with eventual attacks not only on how the spaghetti will be prepared but also on one spouse's character as well as the other spouse's relatives.

According to the Maces, after a series of these heartrending interchanges over a period of months and years, partners grow fearful of intimacy. Revealing their frustrations and insecurities, they come to believe, could render them more vulnerable in future arguments. Eventually, both parties clam up and withdraw from the fray. Their sex life becomes less satisfying. The couple remains married legally, but not emotionally.

Other marriages with one or more hostile partners can have a different problem, the Maces report. In these marriages, anger is almost never expressed by one spouse, whereas the other heartlessly rides roughshod over the first—always insisting on his or her way, with the other party meekly acquiescing. One partner withdraws emotionally if not physically, investing little or no energy in communicating. A sense of basic trust no longer exists, and couples no longer share insecurities in heart-to-heart talks. Although these couples may not be observed having a lot of angry confrontations, their marriage is a far cry from the dream of true intimacy they expected when they married.

The psychological effects of hostility extend beyond the individual and his or her spouse to include other family members. According to another study by Smith, hostile people perceive less support and more conflict within their families.

Nor are hostile persons good sources of support themselves. Everyone agrees that physical aggression against children is clearly harmful, but in recent years the pernicious effects of even less overt forms of child abuse, such as verbal abuse, have been widely documented.

Hostile personalities also report more difficulties at work. In a study at a financial management firm of seventy-five men and women whose average age was forty, hostile individuals reported greater stress in interpersonal aspects of work, less job satisfaction, and a negative view of work relationships.

In another study of middle-class working women in Lawrence, Kansas, women with high hostility levels reported more stressful job experiences and more daily stresses and tensions. They experienced more role conflict and felt that their skills were being underutilized.

Much of the evidence of the psychological effects of hostility are self-reports. As a result, we don't actually know if relationships truly are usually objectively worse for hostile people. I suspect that they are. From his studies, Smith has been encouraged to believe that hostile people affect the people around them through their aggressive behaviors, thus exacerbating conflicts.

How much do hostile individuals actually achieve at work? The hostile person's need to be in control can be helpful, but only as long as one person can do all the work. As the middle-management level is reached, the complexity and demands of many jobs become too much for one person to handle alone. Others must be recruited, inspired, and educated if the broader, more complex tasks are to be mastered.

For the hostile person unable to trust others' ability to do their jobs competently, this can pose an insurmountable barrier. The job becomes too much to do alone; at the same time, the hostile person's abrasive, aggressive interpersonal style sabotages the very loyalty and commitment that subordinates must have if the work goals are to be met.

This is why the ranks of middle management swell with hostile persons who have reached their level of incompetency—and also why the ranks of upper management contain a large portion of nonhostile leaders whose ability to motivate and inspire others has singled them out for higher things.

Meyer Friedman, the originator of the Type A concept, interviewed 106 national leaders over an eight-year period. Although he found more Type A's than B's, other considerations are needed to interpret the statistics in the accompanying table on page 43.

Friedman himself thinks that the B's actually have an advantage, as he suspects that in the general population more men are Type A than are Type B—as high as three out of four in urban populations. Also, because the Type A concept includes individuals characterized by either time urgency or hostility or both, some of this Type A sample may not have been hostile.

Taken in sum, the evidence is clear: To be happy with your marriage, family, and work, keep hostility in check.

My certainty that hostility can damage health is strengthened still further by a consideration of social, biological, and behavioral mechanisms that are active among hostile persons.

THE HOSTILITY STORY:
SOCIAL ISOLATION HURTS

Hostile folks like our fictional Martin are not mere passive vessels in their social environment. Quite often, hostile persons influence the people they encounter in ways that cause others to

TYPE OF LEADERS	TOTAL NUMBER	TYPE A BEHAVIOR	TYPE B BEHAVIOR
1. University Presidents	11	6 (55%)	5 (45%)
2. Bank Presidents	5	3 (60%)	2 (40%)
3. Corporation Chairmen	30	21 (70%)	9 (30%)
4. Generals, Admirals	11	6 (55%)	5 (45%)
5. Archbishops, Bishops, Rabbis	4	2 (50%)	2 (50%)
6. Journalists, Publishers	22	16 (73%)	6 (27%)
7. Nobel Laureates	11	6 (55%)	5 (45%)
8. Congressmen, Senators	7	3 (43%)	4 (57%)
9. Federal Judges	5	2 (40%)	3 (60%)
TOTAL:	**106**	**65 (61%)**	**41 (39%)**

SOURCE: Meyer Friedman and Diane Ulmer, *Treating Type A Behavior—and Your Heart* (New York: Knopf, 1984), 81–82.

fulfill their cynical, pessimistic expectations. This, in turn, ratchets up their anger still further—thereby making the social environment of the hostile person more stressful than that of the more trusting person. If Martin, for example, had not behaved so aggressively by flashing his lights at the other driver, maybe the other driver would have been more inclined to slow down and let Martin pull in. In other words, Martin's cynical expectations, the anger they engendered in him, and his resulting behavior may have actually *caused* the other driver to behave in a manner that Martin interpreted as mistreatment.

Their cynical mistrust and aggressive behaviors often isolate hostile persons from sources of social support that could help to ameliorate the harmful consequences of hostility. Martin's angry visage and gruff treatment of their son led his wife to withdraw rather than to interact with him in a way that could calm his stress or try to help him curb his risky smoking habit. It should come as no surprise that hostile people have reported that their contacts with others are less satisfying than those of nonhostile people.

A considerable body of research documents the health-damaging effects of such isolation from social support. Dr. George Kaplan and his colleagues have been following several thousand healthy residents of Alameda County, California, for several years. Those residents with fewer social ties had higher death rates than those who were more closely connected to other people and groups. Dr. Dan Blazer, one of my colleagues at Duke, found that those elderly residents of Durham, North Carolina, who reported higher satisfaction with their social contacts live longer than those reporting lower levels of satisfaction. Even social contact with pets can be health enhancing: Recovering heart patients with a pet at home had fewer complications than those living alone.

Along with colleagues in Cardiology at Duke, we recently examined the effects of social ties on survival in more than 1,300 patients we had evaluated here in the late 1970s. Among unmarried patients who told us that they had no one to whom they could confide major concerns, 50 percent were dead within five years. In marked contrast, only 17 percent were dead among patients who were married, reported they had a confidant, or both. This profound impact of social isolation on survival in our heart patients could not be explained by their underlying heart condition. Clearly, the lack of social ties increased the risk of dying for all patients, no matter how severe their disease.

Because hostile people are likely to be more socially isolated than their nonhostile counterparts, a lack of social support is one pathway to disease for hostile persons. It remains to be shown just how social isolation harms health. One possibility is that persons lacking social ties are less likely to have good health habits—recall Martin's wife's not bothering to remind him to stop smoking. With no one to remind them, socially isolated persons may not seek medical attention in a timely way or even remember to take prescribed medicine.

Social isolation may also impose increased stress that might have harmful biological consequences. Among persons living near the Three Mile Island nuclear facility in Pennsylvania after the 1979 accident there, Andrew Baum, a psychologist, found that those reporting lower levels of social support excreted higher levels of stress hormones in their urine. Conversely, having a confidant with whom to share concerns could reduce the biologic impact of stress. For example, another psychologist, James Pennebaker, found that persons given an opportunity to talk with another person about a stressful life event experienced a reduction in blood pressure.

Because disease and death always involve changes in our body's biologic functioning, let's now ask the question: Are there biologic characteristics of hostile persons that might account for their increased health problems?

THE HOSTILITY STORY: OUR BIOLOGY NEEDS TO CATCH UP WITH THE MODERN WORLD

Primates more or less like humans have been around for at least the past *two million years.* Throughout 99.5 percent of human history, an ability to mobilize the body rapidly for fight or flight increased one's chances of surviving and of begetting offspring. This well-developed, ingrained capacity to mobilize our metabolism and physiology—for a description of what happens during a fight-or-flight response, turn back to the story of Martin and read once again about what was going on inside his body—for emergency action is still useful when we need to respond to a real threat to life and limb. But such threats are exceedingly rare in modern society. Unfortunately for Martin and others like him, our low threshold for eliciting a fight-or-flight response is more likely to damage our health than to help us function successfully in today's less danger-ous world. Instead of enjoying a higher chance of surviving an encounter with a sabre-toothed tiger or male rival, the hostile per-son—yes, this includes women too, as we shall see—in the modern world may well be at higher risk of dying as the result of too many unnecessary fight-or-flight responses.

At first, research on biologic mechanisms of stress in heart disease focused on the biologic responses of Type A versus Type B men to various laboratory "stressors," such as mental arithmetic or video games. In 1982, my colleagues and I published such a study in the journal *Science.* Compared with Type B men, while perform-ing mental arithmetic for a prize, Type A men showed larger in-creases in blood flow to their muscles (indicating a bigger fight-or-flight response) as well as increased blood levels of several stress hormones (adrenaline, noradrenaline, and cortisol).

This was very encouraging to us at the time, for it showed that Type A men had more pronounced biologic responses to stress that could be responsible for their increased coronary risk. By this time I was very interested in the biologic consequences of hostility as well and was disappointed to find that Ho scores were unrelated to biologic reactivity to the mental arithmetic task in this study.

Reasoning that mental arithmetic problems might not be the appropriate stimulus to arouse the ire of hostile persons, we soon did another study in which subjects with high Ho scores were interrupted twice by an obnoxious lab technician while they were performing another lab task. Although the "high Ho" subjects tended to rate their anger at the interruption higher and their higher anger ratings were associated with larger muscle blood flow increases, there was no *direct* association in this study between high Ho scores and greater physiologic responses.

Very soon after this only partially successful study, however, we were able to document enhanced biologic reactivity to stress among hostile persons, but *only when they are angered.* This study was the brainchild of Dr. Ed Suarez, a psychologist who was doing a postdoctoral fellowship with me at the time. Ed developed a method of harassing our high and low Ho subjects that was more realistic and believable than the approach we had used in the earlier study.

Imagine yourself a subject in Ed's study. You enter the lab, and the experimenter begins describing what's going to happen. After a while a research assistant comes in and says something to the experimenter, but in a rather gruff and abrupt manner. "He sure got up on the wrong side of the bed this morning," you probably say to yourself.

Later on, after you have been hooked up to blood-pressure cuffs and electrodes to monitor your heart and blood-vessel responses to a "mental task," you begin performing the task—it could be some arithmetic problems—trying to go fast to win a prize offered to the subject with the best performance. Every two minutes or so that same research assistant says over an intercom, "You now have X minutes to go before the end of the task." This goes along quite well for a while, but on a few occasions the assistant criticizes your responses by saying, perhaps, "Quit mumbling, I can't understand what you're saying!"

This is what happens if you happen to be in the "harass"

condition of this study. If you had been assigned to the "non-harass" condition, the technician (who murmured only a pleasantry when he came in before the study) would simply call out the time remaining every two minutes.

How do you feel? Even though this is only an experiment in a laboratory, have you ever encountered such rude people before—in supermarket lines, in traffic, at the office, even among your own circle of friends and family? And are your feelings—surprise, annoyance, anger, fear, whatever—similar to those you have experienced in these "real life" situations?

The feelings of the folks in Ed's study were "real." This is because the "sting" before the study began prevented all but a few from realizing that the obnoxious research assistant was part of the study design. Of course, we informed everyone at the end of the study that the nasty remarks were not directed at them but had been a part of the study only. Those who participated in Ed's study were able to understand that just as researchers interested in the physiological effects of physical exercise must have the subjects in their experiments run on a treadmill, so must researchers wishing to learn about the physiological accompaniments of anger devise ways to have their subjects experience such emotions.

Ed's ingenious scam worked dramatically. When men with high Ho scores were harassed while trying to perform a mental task, they reported much higher levels of anger and irritation afterward than their low Ho–scoring counterparts. In addition, their blood pressure, the blood flow to their muscles, and (in a later similar study) their stress hormones all increased more in response to harassment.

In this study Ed also found that as anger and irritation increased, blood-pressure and muscle blood flow responses increased *only* among the high Ho men; there was no association between anger and irritation and physiologic reactivity in the low Ho men. This was a very important finding, because it told us that only for the hostile person is the emotion of anger a poison. Salt causes increased blood pressure in patients with high blood pressure, but it has no effect on the blood pressure of healthy people. Similarly, anger causes increased blood pressure for the hostile person but has no effect on the blood pressure of nonhostile persons.

Other researchers have made similar observations. For example, Dr. David Shapiro and his colleagues at UCLA studied stress in ambulance workers. Workers with high Ho scores showed larger blood-pressure increases during angry interchanges with emergency-room personnel than did those with low Ho scores.

The tighter link between angry emotions and physiologic hyperreactivity could explain why hostile persons have more health problems. *It also suggests that it may be very important for the hostile person who wants to avoid those health problems to learn how to control his or her anger.*

I wrote "his or her" in that last sentence because Ed Suarez has now done another study using high and low Ho–scoring women and found that, like their male counterparts, high Ho women show greater physiologic reactivity when harassed than do low Ho women. In this study Ed also found that low Ho women who were taking birth-control pills were just as hyperreactive to harassment as the high Ho women. If confirmed in larger studies, these results could mean that oral contraceptives may cancel out some of the protection enjoyed by nonhostile women. Because his first study involved only a few women, Ed is now embarked on an extensive five-year research program to increase our understanding of the biologic mechanisms of hostility—especially as affected by oral contraceptive use—in women.

We have also found that this increased physiologic reactivity to stress is present among high Ho subjects not only when they are being harassed in our lab but also when they are going about their normal daily activities. Consequently, men with high Ho scores show a larger increase of adrenaline in their urine from overnight to daytime than do those with low Ho scores. Paralleling the correlation between anger and physiologic reactivity in the lab studies, the increase in adrenaline excretion was most pronounced in those hostile men who reported increased irritation levels during the daytime.

Another very recent finding from our research into biologic mechanisms of hostility suggests that hostility can *magnify* the impact of another important risk factor, blood *cholesterol,* thereby making a high cholesterol level even worse for a hostile person. Among middle-aged men with high Ho scores, those with higher blood cholesterol levels secreted more adrenaline while performing mental tasks than did those with lower blood cholesterol levels. In contrast, among men with low Ho scores there was an inverse association between blood cholesterol levels and adrenaline responses to the task—as cholesterol levels rose, the adrenaline responses diminished.

Hostile men with high cholesterol, then, are more likely to have *larger* adrenaline responses to stress—a combination that compounds the likelihood of arteriosclerotic plaque buildup in their coronary arteries. In contrast, the *smaller* adrenaline responses we saw in nonhostile men with high cholesterol can be expected to attenuate the effect of their high cholesterol to cause arteriosclerotic plaque buildup.

It would take a long time to prove that this combination of high cholesterol and larger adrenaline responses in hostile men is actually accelerating the development of arteriosclerosis in humans. We would have to measure cholesterol levels and adrenaline responses to a mental arithmetic task in a large number of men in order to ensure a large enough pool of men who develop heart disease during a reasonable follow-up period. Then, we would have to follow them for at least five to ten years to see if those with *both* high cholesterol and larger adrenaline responses were the ones most likely to develop heart disease.

Another, quicker way to test the toxic potential of the high cholesterol/adrenaline combination is to create this same combination in an animal species that develops arteriosclerosis. Ordinary white laboratory rats are quite resistant to developing arteriosclerosis, even when given large amounts of cholesterol. The arteries of Egyptian sand rats, which ordinarily eat only vegetarian fare, develop severe arteriosclerotic plaques when they are fed a diet containing 5 percent cholesterol. When they are fed the 5 percent cholesterol diet alone, it takes six to eight months for these rats to develop arteriosclerotic lesions.

In a second study we implanted beneath the skin of the sand rats capsules that maintained high levels of noradrenaline (another stress hormone with effects very much like those of adrenaline) in the blood at all times. Sand rats with the high noradrenaline levels developed advanced lesions after only two months on the diet.

These results make the case, at least for the sand rat version of arteriosclerosis, that the combination of high cholesterol and larger stress hormone responses we observed in hostile men is indeed capable of speeding the development of arteriosclerotic lesions in arterial walls.

Several known effects of adrenaline and noradrenaline are

probably responsible for their arteriosclerosis-promoting effects. First, they cause the blood pressure to rise and the heart to beat more rapidly, and both of these effects could increase risk of damage to the delicate inner lining of arteries. Second, these stress hormones cause fat cells to release fat into the bloodstream; if this fat is not burned up in the course of intense physical exercise, it is converted by the liver into cholesterol, thereby making more cholesterol available in the blood for incorporation into arteriosclerotic plaques. And third, adrenaline and noradrenaline cause the platelets circulating in the blood to become much more "sticky," thereby stimulating them to stick to damaged areas on the artery lining, where they clump and release other chemicals that are believed to stimulate the growth of arteriosclerotic plaques. There are undoubtedly several other effects of stress hormones, some of them yet to be discovered, that cause harm, but these are more than enough to account for considerable mayhem in the bodily economy of hostile persons.

Hostile persons possess at least two other potential biologic characteristics that could be damaging to health: a weak parasympathetic nervous system and a weak immune system.

In contrast to the sympathetic nervous system (SNS), which is the source of the adrenaline and noradrenaline released during the more frequent fight-or-flight responses experienced by hostile persons, the parasympathetic nervous system (PNS) performs a *calming* function. When activated, PNS nerves release the chemical compound acetylcholine into any tissue they supply. Once it makes its way inside a cell anywhere in the body, acetylcholine has the effect of stopping the effects of adrenaline, such as the more rapid and forceful beating of heart-muscle cells. Because most organs involved in the fight-or-flight response—for example, the heart and the arteries—receive input from both the SNS and PNS, it is possible for PNS activation to act as a "brake" on the fight-or-flight physiologic changes caused by SNS activation.

In a series of studies carried out over the past decade in collaboration with colleagues from Tohoku Medical School in Sendai, Japan, we have found that Type A men, particularly those with high Ho scores, show weaker PNS responses than low Ho–scoring Type B men. One way to study how well parts of the nervous system are working is to activate nervous "reflexes." The knee jerk is a good example of such a test, one you've doubtless experienced at your most recent medical checkup. When the tendon attached to the kneecap is stretched by a quick tap, it stimulates sensory nerves that go into the spinal cord, where they connect to and activate motor nerves that go back to the leg muscles, causing the lower leg to jerk upward.

A similar reflex activates the PNS: An ice pack applied to the upper face stimulates sensory nerves that go directly to the base of the brain, where they connect to and activate a PNS nerve, the vagus, that releases acetylcholine in the heart, causing it to slow its rate of beating. When we activated this reflex in Type A men, their heart rate slowed similarly to that of Type B men for the first minute the ice pack was on the face. After two minutes, however, the heart rate had speeded back up in the Type As but had slowed even more in the Type B's, indicating a weaker PNS reflex in the Type A's.

Since a brisk PNS can counter the effects of the SNS in making the heart work harder, thus helping slow the development of coronary disease, a weaker PNS represents yet another way the nervous system of hostile persons might place them at higher risk of developing heart disease.

Finally, there is just beginning to emerge some evidence that the immune system may be weaker in hostile persons. You will recall that in the Western Electric Study, men with high Ho scores tended to be at higher risk of dying, not only from coronary disease but from cancer as well. Although we certainly don't know all we need to know about the causes of cancer, there is a strong indication that the immune system plays an important protective role when it comes to keeping our bodies free of cancer. "Natural killer cells" are cells in the immune system known to have the ability to "kill" tumor cells that form in the body. Many cancer researchers believe them to be a key part of our body's cancer surveillance system, recognizing and killing cancer cells as they form.

It is quite interesting, therefore, that University of Colorado researchers have recently found that, relative to their low Ho-scoring counterparts, medical students with high Ho scores had fewer natural killer cells in their blood during high-stress exam periods. Although the mechanism responsible for this reduction in natural killer cells among the high Ho students isn't known at present, it very likely stems from effects of their increased SNS activation in suppressing the immune system.

In summary, the hostile person's nervous system is "wired" differently from that of the nonhostile person. The SNS is activated by the slightest provocation in the hostile person, whereas in the nonhostile person even strong stimuli cause relatively small SNS responses. And even when nonhostile persons do have a strong SNS response, their relatively strong PNS quickly comes in and terminates the SNS effects in key body tissues. The net effects of this relatively strong SNS and weak PNS in hostile persons—increased cardiovascular activation, increased mobilization of cholesterol into the blood, increased clumping of platelets, and decreased immune system functions, to mention but a few—are quite capable of starting in motion pathological processes that would account for the higher death rates observed among hostile persons in the epidemiologic studies I reviewed earlier.

As I noted at the start of this section, all of these responses would be quite useful if we were still living in the world of our ancestors two million years ago. Considering that we don't have nearly the need for these rapid emergency responses that our distant ancestors did, however, it might be a good idea not to wait for evolutionary processes to weed these "vestigial" responses out of the gene pool. It would be better to take steps now to blunt the harm that our ancient nervous systems are causing for some of us.

Before getting to those steps, however, there is more bad news for us hostile folks.

THE HOSTILITY STORY: WE DON'T EVEN TAKE GOOD CARE OF OURSELVES!

Some of the earlier studies showed that persons with high Ho scores not only suffered more health problems but also engaged in more risky behaviors, such as smoking or alcohol use. These risky behaviors did not explain all the increased health problems among hostile persons, but the observed association has led subsequent researchers to look more closely at the health habits of hostile versus nonhostile persons. The findings only strengthen our impression of hostility as a health-damaging trait.

As I noted earlier in describing the epidemiologic evidence that hostility harms health, the origin of the Ho scale in the widely used MMPI has made it possible to go back to data collected in the past and perform follow-up studies that, if begun now, would take decades to produce any answers. The largest such study now under way is one begun in the 1980s as a collaborative effort between Duke and the University of North Carolina (UNC).

Under the direction of Dr. Ilene Siegler, the UNC Alumni Heart Study (UNCAHS) has now enrolled nearly five thousand former UNC students who took the MMPI as a part of freshman orientation twenty-five years ago. Thank goodness again for Dr. Grant Dahlstrom's "packrat" tendency to save every MMPI ever given at UNC! The UNCAHS participants are now providing, on a yearly basis, ongoing information regarding their current health and health habits.

Although the UNC graduates are still too young to have had enough heart attacks for us to be able to correlate their health with their Ho scores from the college years, we have already found that those participants who had higher Ho scores in college have poorer health *habits* now. Compared with their classmates whose Ho scores had been in the lower range, those with higher-range Ho scores twenty-five years earlier are now more likely to be smokers, to consume more alcohol, to have a larger body mass index (a measure of obesity), to have higher cholesterol levels, and to consume more caffeine. In further analyses of the UNCAHS data, John Barefoot has shown that high Ho scores in college predicted failure to quit smoking among those who had ever smoked. Therefore, higher Ho scores at age eighteen predict more risky behaviors in the early forties.

Dr. Larry Scherwitz and his colleagues also found a similar association between higher Ho scores and risky behaviors in CARDIA, another large-scale study of eighteen- to thirty-year-old men and women who recently provided information about risk factors and completed the Ho scale. Those with higher Ho scores were more likely to be smokers but did not have higher body mass indexes or higher cholesterol levels. They did eat more, however; those whose Ho scores were in the upper quarter consumed *six hundred more calories* per day than those with Ho scores in the lowest quarter. Because the participants in this study are younger than those in the UNCAHS, it may be that their tendency to overeat has not yet had sufficient impact on their weight and cholesterol levels to cause the elevations we found among middle-aged UNCAHS participants.

WHAT MAKES US HOSTILE?
SOME SPECULATIONS ON
THE NEUROCHEMICAL BASIS OF
THE HOSTILITY SYNDROME

I have now described a broad range of characteristics—both behavioral and biological—that cluster together in persons who score high on the Ho scale. Persons with high Ho scores report more anger and aggressive tendencies. They appear to eat, drink, and smoke more. They exhibit stronger responses of the sympathetic nervous system, the branch that mediates the fight-or-flight response, and weaker responses of the parasympathetic nervous system, the branch that blunts and slows the effects of the sympathetic branch on bodily tissues and organs. I will refer to this cluster of characteristics found among persons scoring high on the Ho scale as the Hostility Syndrome. The word *syndrome* is apt because it implies that this cluster of characteristics may have a common source or cause.

Of course, much research will be required before we can identify such a cause. Obviously, how children are treated by their parents and other caregivers plays an important role in the development of the cynical expectations that fuel the anger and aggressive tendencies of the hostile person. There can be little question that nurturing—or its absence—is critical to the emergence of the hostile personality. Research on identical twins suggests, however, that nature—the influence of our genes on brain functions—is an equal contributor to many aspects of adult personality, including hostility.

Ultimately, all behavior is mediated by brain functions, and brain functions depend on chemicals called neurotransmitters that are released by nerves to affect the functioning of other nerves. Lower or higher levels of a single neurotransmitter could be responsible for many of the characteristics making up the Hostility Syndrome. Demonstration of such a neurochemical basis would suggest that the Hostility Syndrome is the result of particular patterns of neurotransmitter function—and therefore possibly genetically determined.

Some evidence already points to a single neurotransmitter as the possible cause of the Hostility Syndrome. The first column of the accompanying table lists the components of the Hostility Syndrome, as revealed by the research described here. The right column summarizes evidence from a broad range of research, mostly in biological psychiatry, showing that each component in the left column *could be* the result of deficiency in the brain of the neurotransmitter serotonin. Researchers have already found, for example, that persons with a history of aggressive behaviors have reduced levels of the major breakdown product of serotonin in the fluid bathing their brain and spinal cord—suggesting an association between low serotonin function and aggressive behavior.

Other research, mainly on animals, has shown that stimulation of a certain class of serotonin receptors in the brain causes a decrease in the output of the sympathetic nervous system and an increase in the output of the parasympathetic nervous system. Therefore, low serotonin function could be expected to increase sympathetic output and decrease parasympathetic output—the same pattern observed in hostile persons. By feeding cats the

---

The components that make up the Hostility Syndrome and the effects of lowered brain serotonin on those components.

HOSTILITY SYNDROME COMPONENT	EFFECT OF LOWERED BRAIN SEROTONIN
High irritability and aggression	Increased aggressive behavior
Increased sympathetic nervous system activity	Increased sympathetic nervous system activity
Decreased parasympathetic nervous system activity	Decreased parasympathetic nervous system activity
Increased smoking	Possible increase in pleasurable effects of nicotine and smoking
Increased eating and weight gain	Increased eating and weight gain
Increased alcohol consumption	Increased alcohol consumption

serotonin precursor tryptophan, Richard Verrier, a Georgetown University physiologist, documented directly that raising brain serotonin levels causes a reduction in the firing rate of SNS nerves going to the heart.

Both animal and human studies have documented that raising brain serotonin causes subjects to eat less and lose weight, whereas reducing brain serotonin causes them to eat more and gain weight. This association is a likely explanation for the tendency of persons with high Ho scores in CARDIA and the UNCAHS to eat more, weigh more, and have higher cholesterol levels as they grow older.

Some evidence suggests that even the act of eating itself causes release of serotonin within the brain. If this is so, then Martin's overeating after the stressful drive home could have been an attempt to calm himself by raising the dose of serotonin delivered to some receptors in his brain.

The rewarding properties of nicotine appear to depend upon stimulation of a specific serotonin receptor in the brain, and enhancement of brain serotonin levels by tryptophan treatment has been reported to help people who are trying to quit smoking. Dr. Bonnie Spring has found that giving a drug that enhances brain serotonin function to smokers who have stopped helps keep them from gaining weight. Low brain serotonin function, then, may promote smoking and/or make it harder to stop, either directly or via side effects such as unwanted weight gain. As with the UNCAHS participants with high Ho scores who tended to weigh more, the smokers with high Ho scores are more likely to be unable to quit smoking because of a weaker brain serotonin system.

Finally, reduced levels of a serotonin breakdown product are found in the fluid bathing the brain and spinal cord of alcoholics, suggesting that low serotonin function in the brain may predispose them to drink more alcohol. A strain of rats with a genetically determined preference to drink alcohol over water that are treated with the serotonin-enhancing drug fluoxetine (well known as Prozac) drink less alcohol but no less water. Could it be that, as with their eating and smoking behaviors, the tendency of persons with high Ho scores to consume more alcohol is also caused by low brain serotonin function?

Although completely circumstantial, the evidence cited does suggest with some consistency that low brain serotonin function is a *biologically plausible explanation* for all the characteristics that cluster to make up the Hostility Syndrome. We might even someday begin to think of hostile persons as having—relative to nonhostile persons—a "serotonin deficiency disorder." More research will be required to provide direct evidence for this hypothesis. Given the rapidly growing number of drugs designed to increase brain serotonin function, confirmation of this hypothesis would not only enlighten us regarding the biologic basis of the Hostility Syndrome and its health-damaging effects but could also point the way to exciting prevention and treatment programs for hostile people.

In contrast to the drastic means—a bullet in the brain—used to reduce Henry's hostility in the movie *Regarding Henry,* one or more of these new "serotonergic" drugs could turn out to be a real "magic bullet" for reducing hostility while doing little or no harm.

If the research just now starting is successful in showing that low serotonin function lies at the heart of the Hostility Syndrome, it may have the added benefit of making us all—hostile and nonhostile alike—a bit more tolerant of both ourselves and others with that syndrome. For then we should be able to see that hostility is not something that one obstinately chooses but rather something that stems from a person's neurochemical makeup—hardly a reason for blaming.

But identifying the genetic/neurochemical basis for the Hostility Syndrome and using this knowledge to develop a pharmacologic "magic bullet" to protect us from its ravages is far in the future. For the present, as we shall see in the next chapter and the rest of this book, there are already available effective *behavior modification* approaches that not only reduce hostility and anger but also improve health. Our hostility may be bred in our genes, but this does not mean that we are helpless to blunt its harmful effects. We need not look to medicine for all the answers, however.

And even if a serotonergic magic bullet becomes available, we will almost surely still want to use it in conjunction with these same behavior modification approaches. It is already becoming clear, for example, that although these serotonergic drugs help people stop smoking, they are less effective by themselves than when combined with behavioral approaches.

So it will be important for you to learn about the behavioral approaches to hostility reduction that form the bulk of this book. Without them, it is doubtful that even a pharmacologic magic bullet will be sufficient to protect you from the ravages of your hostility. Besides, these behavior modification approaches really do work.

IS IT POSSIBLE TO REDUCE
HOSTILITY; WILL DOING SO IMPROVE
MY HEALTH?

Cardiologists and others concerned about heart disease devote much appropriate attention to reducing the traditional risk factors—smoking, high cholesterol, and high blood pressure. Reducing risk factors is good preventive medicine.

Not surprising, the evidence that the Hostility Syndrome is bad for your health is less extensive than that available for these established risk factors. Nevertheless, you have several good reasons to change hostile behaviors and attitudes.

- Most of the available evidence suggests that hostile people are at higher risk for cardiovascular disease (as well as other illnesses) for a variety of reasons, including reduced social support, increased biologic reactivity when angered, and increased indulgence in risky health behaviors.

- There is little reason to be concerned that reducing your hostility is going to cause you any harm.

- Finally, research has already documented that some behavioral treatment approaches designed to reduce patients' hostility and to increase social ties do lead to their improved health.

Dr. Meyer Friedman, in addition to his work showing that Type A behavior predicts increased coronary risk, has completed a second pioneering study, the Recurrent Coronary Prevention Project (RCPP). In this study, Friedman and his colleagues enrolled one thousand men who had had recent heart attacks into a program in which two-thirds were randomly assigned to a treatment program designed to reduce all aspects of their Type A behavior, with a strong emphasis on curbing their hostility and anger. The other third received routine care from their cardiologist. After four years, the group receiving behavior modification training to reduce Type A behavior had suffered fewer recurrent heart attacks and other heart problems.

More recently, Dr. Dean Ornish has completed an ambitious study that produced similar, equally encouraging results. Subjects were forty-one heart patients with coronary artery blockages severe enough to cause their heart muscles to be starved for blood. These patients were randomly assigned to routine cardiology care or to a comprehensive treatment program that included dietary fat restriction, exercise, yogic relaxation training, and group sessions designed to improve their ability to cope with stress. Compared with the nineteen subjects in the routine care group, the twenty-two in the special intervention group showed actual shrinkage of their coronary artery lesions and improved heart-muscle function—without drugs or surgery. In addition to the benefits of diet, meditation, and exercise, Ornish feels strongly that the patients' improved ability to handle stress, which he ascribes to the social support provided by the group sessions, was a key ingredient in the treatment program's success.

Other studies support this idea. In a Montreal study of heart attack victims conducted by Dr. Nancy Frasure-Smith, some patients were randomly assigned to receive routine care. Those in another group of patients were called by a nurse each month, in addition to their regular treatment. On these calls, the nurses asked the patients how they were faring. If the patient indicated any problems, the nurse visited to try to help resolve the difficulty. The patients receiving this extra "social support" had both fewer deaths and fewer recurrent heart attacks than the group that received routine care.

The results in this study recall our finding at Duke of very high death rates in unmarried heart patients with no one to confide in. The presence of a spouse or confidant very likely served the same purpose in improving survival as the nurse who called to check on the Montreal patients and help them cope with problems. As Pennebaker has noted, the opportunity to share major concerns with another human being has a broad range of salutary effects.

Equally encouraging is another study that was begun by Dr. David Spiegel of Stanford University with the express intention of debunking the notion hyped by many "new age" types that having positive thoughts about your cancer can improve your chances of survival. Spiegel randomly assigned women with advanced metastatic breast cancer to either routine care or routine care plus a cancer patient support group. Patients in the support group were provided a safe and caring setting in which they could discuss the issues they all faced. Despite Spiegel's expectation that, although the support group might improve patients' mood, it would have no effect on their survival, the women assigned to the support group survived twice as long—eighteen months compared with nine months—as the women in the routine care group.

Considered together, these studies provide good evidence that reducing your hostility and anger and becoming more connected to other people *will improve your health.*

SOME FINAL THOUGHTS

You have now completed a "crash course" on hostility. Here are the key points to take with you.

1. Hostile people—those with high levels of cynicism, anger, and aggression—are at higher risk of developing life-threatening illness than are their less hostile counterparts.

2. By driving others away, or by not perceiving the support they could be deriving from their social contacts, hostile people may be depriving themselves of the health-enhancing, stress-buffering benefits of social support.

3. A quicker activation of their fight-or-flight response, in combination with their relatively weak parasympathetic calming response, is a biologic mechanism that probably contributes to the health problems that afflict hostile people.

4. Hostile people also are more prone to engage in a number of risky behaviors—eating more, drinking more alcohol, smoking— that could damage their health.

5. In the future we may achieve a better understanding of the genetic and neurochemical basis of the Hostility Syndrome. This understanding will likely focus on the role of the brain's serotonin system. At present there are already available behavioral approaches that appear effective in ameliorating its harmful effects.

If the self-assessment you did in chapter 1 showed you to be among those whose hostility level imposes a risk to your health—not to mention, of course, your important interpersonal relationships— and if you are convinced of that risk by the scientific evidence I have presented in this chapter, you are now ready to begin mastering the survival skills described in the rest of this book.

PART III
SURVIVAL SKILLS

Congratulations. You are still reading. This means you remain open to acknowledging your hostility, reexamining your own behavior, and considering new ways of responding to stressful situations. Your attitude bodes well, as this in itself appears to protect you against disease in general. That is, individuals who have strong feelings of confidence in their ability to control circumstances, a willingness to see life events as challenges rather than as obstacles, and a strong commitment to the experiences and demands of daily living have fewer illnesses than those who lack these qualities.

Hostility can be conquered by a number of different strategies, each of which we'll discuss in a different chapter.

Two sets of strategies will help you control hostility by getting rid of the negative stimulus—the person or situation that sets you off in the first place. Using your reasoning powers, you may be able to redefine the anger-invoking situation as not an important threat (chapter 3). On other occasions, you can snuff out the negative stimulus by deflection strategies (chapters 4 through 7). By removing the anger-producing stimuli, or dampening responsiveness, you can cut off the cascade of physiological responses before your cardiovascular system is overstimulated.

There will be times when you *are* being mistreated and need to do something about it. Chapter 8, which deals with assertion, presents ways to act effectively when you choose to remain angry.

Another set of strategies is designed primarily to change you rather than the stimulus. When you improve your relationships with others, you'll find yourself in fewer anger-invoking situations (chapters 9 through 16). Adopting a better attitude toward life has a similar effect, by switching your emphasis from anger-invoking negative situations to a more positive focus (chapters 17 through 19).

Many strategies presented here work on more than one level.

Humor can help you adopt a more positive philosophy; it's also useful for defusing specific crises. Listening, increasing empathy, practicing tolerance, forgiveness, and pretending that each day is your last can help you improve your relationships with others, but they also can help you reason with yourself and deflect anger.

Each chapter deals with a single strategy, following a common outline. We start with "General Principles"—"When to Use This Strategy," "How to Use This Strategy," and "Why This Strategy Works." We next offer some examples—from a variety of sources, including literature, Redford's experiences with patients, and our own personal experiences—to illustrate how the strategy might work or why it is needed. We then present the "ABCs" of each strategy which summarize the key points. Finally, we conclude each chapter with some exercises you can do to improve your ability to use that chapter's strategy.

This book is firmly grounded in a broad range of scientific findings, as well as personal experiences. Understanding this accumulated wisdom is a first, but only a beginning, step. Your constant focus must be on actually changing your behavior.

Because conquering your hostility involves basic changes in your thoughts and actions, you must commit yourself to practicing over and over again new patterns of behavior. Lowering your hostility does not mean wiping out all your hostile attitudes, thoughts, and actions with one great eradication but gradually replacing this pattern of behavior with a healthier one. You will probably find lowering your high hostility levels hard work at first, but these small initial gains are important. Eventually these gains become cumulative. If you stay with these strategies, biological patterns of behavior you may have been born with will no longer rule you, any more than you will be controlled by your past.

To get the most out of this book, relate the strategy under discussion to your own situation as often as you can. From working on our own hostility, we know what angers us. Following are a couple of our pet peeves you'll see illustrated by various incidents throughout our book.

- *Redford's Pet Peeve #1:* Bad drivers. (Example: The driver pulls onto the highway, crosses in front of me to get to my fast lane, and then slows down.) Traffic is a common trigger of anger in hostile folks. In a column he wrote about *The Trusting Heart,* George F. Will described his rage at drivers who get in the left lane at a stoplight planning to turn left and don't turn on the turn signal—causing him to get stuck behind them!

- *Virginia's Pet Peeve #1:* Self-centered people. (Example: I am describing an incident. The other person interrupts me in midstory to describe her own, only vaguely related experience.)

Our pet peeves aren't necessarily what rile you most frequently and intensely, so focusing on our illustrations won't be enough to enable you to conquer most of your own hostility. Instead, focus most closely on the problems *you* frequently face that enrage *you* the most. So what will it be—how your spouse, offspring, or other relatives behave? Your lazy, incompetent, or glory-stealing co-workers? How other people treat your children? Your inconsiderate boss? Government officials? Other countries? Incompetents? Lazy individuals? How your money is spent? Authors insensitive enough to presume to guess what ticks you off?

Before you read the next chapter, look over your entries in your Hostility Log. Use these entries as well as more free-ranging reflections to identify the three pet peeves that annoy you most frequently or irritate you most, and list them in the spaces provided below. As you read the chapters ahead, you can be thinking of how you might use the strategies being described to help you cope better with your pet peeves.

As you get started on your program of learning to reduce your hostility, we propose that you commit to an *initial trial period* during which you will work diligently on the strategies we'll be describing. We recognize that to maintain continuity and your interest, you may need to proceed at a faster pace than you might if you were taking our workshop. On the other hand, our experiences helping groups of people to overcome their cynicism, anger, and aggression suggest that a couple of months of initial practice is ideal. We therefore recommend at least a four-week trial. During this period,

- You'll probably prefer to read the chapters one by one, focusing on each strategy for a while before going on to another chapter.

- Promise yourself that for this period you will keep your Hostility Log. (We know that some of you will find this hard to do every day. You need to understand, however, that your ability to use the strategies will improve more quickly if you do keep the Log at least every other day.)

- Set aside a regularly scheduled amount of practice time each day. Spend this practice time carrying out the exercises we provide in the last section of each chapter or developing your meditation skills. Practicing fifteen minutes a day five days a week during your initial commitment period is reasonable, but you may prefer to devote more or less time than that. What is most important is to decide on your time commitment and stick to it.

- Commit yourself to trying to apply what you are learning throughout each day.

FIRST PET PEEVE

_____
_____
_____
_____
_____

SECOND PET PEEVE

_____
_____
_____
_____
_____

THIRD PET PEEVE

_____
_____
_____
_____
_____

By the time your initial period of commitment is up, you will have given yourself a fair chance to begin the process of change. You can then assess whether you want to continue for another four weeks. We bet you will!

Two rules to live by:
1. Don't sweat the small stuff.
2. Most matters are small stuff!

Reprinted with special permission of King Features Syndicate.

Many of the hostile person's problems begin with inappropriate thoughts about other people or situations that can't be changed. By learning to reason with yourself, you can often talk yourself out of cynical thoughts, angry feelings, and aggressive behaviors. This skill is one you will use as the starting point for all the strategies that follow.

CHAPTER 3

Reason with Yourself

"Anger is never without a reason, but seldom with a good one."   Benjamin Franklin,
Poor Richard's Almanac, 1754

GENERAL PRINCIPLES.

When to Use This Strategy

Your toddler plants footprints all over the floor you've just finished mopping. You want to scream. In almost every such situation, your best first strategy is to *reason with yourself.* Many times, you will talk yourself out of your anger. If you need to take additional action to overcome your hostility or to act effectively, you'll already have gathered enough information to choose among the other strategies in your hostility survival kit.

Courtesy Raleigh News and Observer

How to Use This Strategy

Basically, you are going to try to talk yourself out of being upset, if your rational examination of the situation leads you to the conclusion that your initial cynical thought, angry feeling, or urge to act aggressively was inappropriate. As soon as you succeed in talking yourself out of being angry, simply drop the matter.

Refer to the Hostility Roadmap (figure 3.1). Let's examine the various questions again, this time adding the step of following up your no answers by reasoning with yourself.

To begin, enter into a dialogue with yourself in which you consider the objective facts of the situation that stimulated the initial hostile thought, feeling, or action. In this dialogue, consider only what you can actually observe, not what you infer about someone else's motives. After this objective examination, refer again to your Roadmap to decide if the situation is worth your continued attention. Yes, the traffic light has changed twice and you've yet to drive through the intersection, but you'll still get to work on time. Why are you turning the delay into a big deal? Do you have better ways to spend your time than being upset? Whenever you could be better occupied, reason with yourself that, even though your ire is justified, the whole situation is too unimportant to be worth bothering with. Your time is too valuable to waste on so petty a matter. You can take control, refuse to measure out your life in droplets of spleen.

In most situations, you can decide on the basis of the objective evidence whether you have enough information to evaluate the situation. If you do, you can almost always conclude whether your hostile thoughts and feelings are justified or not. Whenever you conclude that your anger isn't justified or that you lack the necessary evidence to decide, try to talk yourself out of being upset.

You have deduced that your cat had jumped on top of your bookcase, knocking off a glass you left there; was the cat being malevolent or simply behaving like a cat? The latter is more likely.

Rain pours down the day of your long-scheduled party; the weather forecaster had predicted only a 35 percent chance of rain, but is he responsible for the weather? Of course not!

You have just arrived at an unfamiliar train station. The central display clock is broken and you aren't wearing a watch. Has the clock been broken for fifteen minutes or fifteen days? You don't

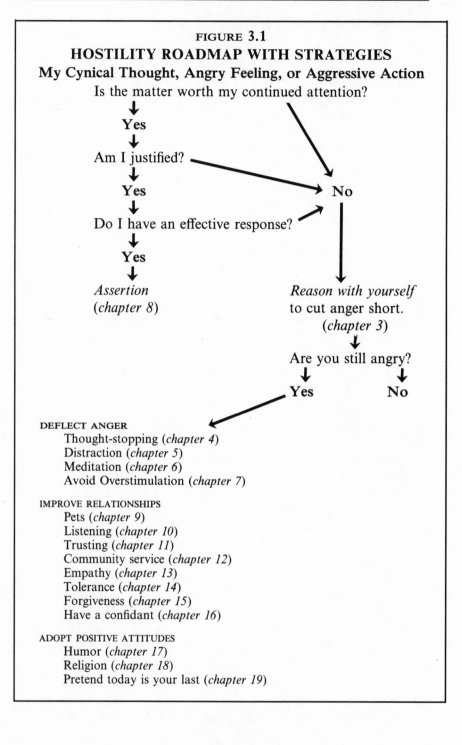

FIGURE **3.1**

HOSTILITY ROADMAP WITH STRATEGIES

My Cynical Thought, Angry Feeling, or Aggressive Action

Is the matter worth my continued attention?

↓

Yes

↓

Am I justified?

↓

Yes → **No**

↓

Do I have an effective response?

↓

Yes

↓

Assertion
(chapter 8)

Reason with yourself
to cut anger short.
(chapter 3)

↓

Are you still angry?

Yes   **No**

DEFLECT ANGER
   Thought-stopping *(chapter 4)*
   Distraction *(chapter 5)*
   Meditation *(chapter 6)*
   Avoid Overstimulation *(chapter 7)*

IMPROVE RELATIONSHIPS
   Pets *(chapter 9)*
   Listening *(chapter 10)*
   Trusting *(chapter 11)*
   Community service *(chapter 12)*
   Empathy *(chapter 13)*
   Tolerance *(chapter 14)*
   Forgiveness *(chapter 15)*
   Have a confidant *(chapter 16)*

ADOPT POSITIVE ATTITUDES
   Humor *(chapter 17)*
   Religion *(chapter 18)*
   Pretend today is your last *(chapter 19)*

know the answer to that, so you can't know if anger is justified or not.

On the other hand, you can conclude that the neighbor who for several days in a row allows his dog to perform bodily functions in your yard instead of his is acting inappropriately. The person about to break into the line in front of you at the bus stop may get the last seat, leaving you out in the cold. The inconsiderate boob has more nerve than manners! Your ire is justified.

If you decide that the situation merits your continued attention, that you are justified, or if you feel angry anyway, next ask yourself if you have an effective response available.

Sometimes you can respond effectively. You can ask the inconsiderate neighbor who allows his dog to defecate on your grass not to do that. You can tell the person about to break into the line at the bus stop where the end of the line is located. Score victories for justified anger in situations you consider important when you do have effective options.

Whenever you lack a good response, follow the Roadmap and reason with yourself that uselessly spinning your wheels harms only you. With careful logic, try in your internal dialogue to convince yourself that your response will not change the person (or inanimate object, group, or nation) who first aroused your ire, if that is indeed the case. The weather may be nasty, but your ranting and cursing isn't going to melt the first icicle. The neighbor who has just painted his house tacky green likes that color and he is not in the least interested in hearing your opinion on the subject! You can move or learn to live with the color.

After you finish these three dialogues evaluating the merit, justice, and effectiveness of responding to whatever upset you, refer again to the Roadmap. Ask yourself, "Am I still angry?" If the answer is no, congratulate yourself. You have succeeded in defusing your anger.

When the answer is yes, next think what's going on inside your body right now—if you've forgotten, go back and read about what happened to Martin when he became angry at the driver ahead of him on the road back to Raleigh. If your own health and physical well-being are likely to suffer most from any continued action, reason yourself out of such self-destructive behavior.

Another way to think about reasoning with yourself is to recall those old cartoons at the movies—where a little "devil" would appear on Elmer Fudd's shoulder, saying, "Go ahead! Shoot that wabbit!" When you are having cynical thoughts, it's your own "devil" talking to you.

Now recall how on Elmer Fudd's other shoulder a little "angel" appears, reminding Elmer, "Hey, wait a minute! That wabbit may have a family to support!" If you listen to your own "angel" trying to talk you out of your anger, you may find your hostility ebbing away.

Often, no matter how carefully and well you reason with yourself, you will still be left with the cynical thought, the angry feeling, the aggressive urge. This means it's time to move on to other strategies listed on the Roadmap.

Why This Strategy Works

Once you realize the lack of merit, justice, or your potential to change a situation, your hostility will likely dissipate. Your repetitious internal dialogue will very often simply help the rational parts of your mind dominate over the more ancient parts oriented toward the quick fight-or-flight responses that originally functioned to ensure survival. This delay tactic often succeeds because you are allowing yourself time to examine rationally the overall situation instead of allowing some small stimulus to trigger an inappropriate emotional response.

Let's examine in detail some examples to see how this strategy works. Lawrence is traveling along back roads rather late at night. He is both sleepy and thirsty. A caffeinated cola is called for. He finally spots a drink machine in front of a dimly lit, deserted service station. He pulls in, gets out of his car, and is relieved to find his favorite brand of diet cola as one of the selections. What luck! He fishes around in his rather empty pockets and finally comes up with three quarters, which he quickly deposits in the machine. No cola descends. He kicks the machine. Still no cola. He shakes the machine, again to no avail. Then he sees a sign that he considers to be obscure. "Out of order." "Damn it!" The service station is locked and obviously deserted. He can begin to feel his blood pressure rise.

Time for the Hostility Roadmap (figure 3.1.). The objective facts of the situation are that Lawrence did not see the "Out of Order" sign, he has lost his last three quarters in a broken machine, and no one is there to refund his money. Furthermore, the station probably won't reopen before the next morning. He cannot determine with certainty if the owner had purposefully made the sign obscure or if any sign would have been hard to see in the dim light. And, in fact, he had been in a hurry to get his drink and had missed the sign in part because he was concentrating on coming up with enough change.

Is the matter trivial? Well, maybe most people would find it so. Because he needs that caffeine to stay awake, Lawrence concludes that the matter is important to him.

Is Lawrence's anger justified? Yes, as he has lost seventy-five cents. Mainly, he is still very thirsty.

Lawrence continues to ask the Roadmap questions. Does he have an effective response? He could write the owner of the service station a nasty note demanding a refund. But he doesn't have any paper, and he also would have to locate a pen. All in all, the extra effort he'd have to expend would take another fifteen minutes. Even then the note would probably just blow away. He could write a letter later, but for that he would need an address—more hassle. And he has no assurance that the owner will honor his request for a refund. If after fifteen more minutes of effort, Lawrence didn't get his money back, he'd be even more upset than he is now. He has options, but they are not attractive enough to merit the extra effort and possible extra frustration. Lawrence decides to cut his losses by dropping the matter.

Under different circumstances, Barbara applies the Roadmap to reach a different conclusion than Lawrence. She has just received in the mail a jogging suit she ordered. The color is wrong, and a review of her order slip indicates that the shipper, not she, made the mistake. The incompetents! She can feel her blood pressure rise as she curses them. After a couple minutes of stewing, she remembers her Roadmap strategy.

Barbara first asks herself if the matter is trivial. Yes and no. Surely receiving a jogging suit of the wrong color is unimportant in the big scheme of life. But she does expect to be treated fairly and the mistake is not hers. Barbara next asks herself is her anger is justified. She decides it is.

Barbara therefore considers her options, the last question on her Roadmap. She could put the jogging suit back into the box and return it with a nasty note. But that means either a trip to the post

office or to UPS, with more money out of her pocket. Barbara finds
that she can't think effectively about her options if she stays agi-
tated, so she takes several deep breaths.

Calmer now, Barbara remembers that she still has the catalogue in which she originally saw the suit. Why not call their "800"
number to explain what happened? If the company representative
does not suggest it first, Barbara will request that UPS pick up the
suit at the company's expense and that the company then reprocess
her original order. This is obviously her best option! Now rather
pleased with herself for acting so effectively, Barbara proceeds to
look for the catalogue.

THE ABCS OF REASONING WITH YOURSELF

A. Conduct a Roadmap dialogue with yourself to decide whether
the situation merits your continued attention, whether your
thought/feeling/or urge is justified, and whether you have an effective response.

B. If you answer no to any of these questions and prefer not to be
upset, try to talk yourself out of the thought, feeling, or urge.

C. If you remain angry, next consider if your anger is worth the
biological costs to your health. If necessary, quickly move on to
other strategies listed on the expanded Roadmap.

EXERCISES

1. Add two permanent additional categories to your Hostility Log:

When
Scene
Thought
Feeling
Action
Involvement
Strategy used
Outcome

At the moment, your only strategy is reasoning with yourself, but
you eventually will have additional options. Keeping tabs on what

you tried and what the result was will enable you to review which strategies work most effectively for you under different circumstances.

2. Use the Roadmap dialogue to talk yourself out of being angry under the following circumstances:

A. You and a good friend have been planning a picnic (or boating trip, or tennis game), but the weather suddenly turns bad. You are becoming irritable and snappish.

B. The puppy you are housebreaking pees inside. As you clean up the mess you can feel your heartbeat quicken and your cheeks redden.

C. You stub your toe against the leg of a newly relocated table. Your pride and toe both are hurt!

D. Your colleague's assistant usually arrives at work late, snacks at her desk, and has what you consider to be too many absences. Just seeing her makes your blood pressure rise.

E. Your ex-spouse (or spouse, significant other, or other person in your life) took your child (or niece, nephew, little friend in the apartment complex, or other child important to you) to see the movie you had been planning as a surprise treat.

STRATEGIES TO DEFLECT ANGER

Next to talking yourself out of being angry, the simplest way to control your own cynicism, anger, or aggression is to tune out whatever is causing it. We begin with thought stopping (chapter 4), the quickest technique for erasing hostile thoughts. If that fails, next try distracting yourself (chapter 5). Meditation (chapter 6) is the final deflection strategy. It is more involved than the others, but this strategy is also more likely to be effective. All of these deflection strategies work best when you cut back on or eliminate stimulants and exercise regularly (chapter 7).

CHAPTER 4

Stop Hostile Thoughts, Feelings, and Urges

"... Put them all away: anger, wrath, malice, slander, and foul talk from your mouth."   Colossians 3:8

GENERAL PRINCIPLES

When to Use This Strategy

You have just gone through the questions on your Hostility Roadmap. (This can proceed very quickly once you're familiar with the technique.) You have decided that a hostile thought, feeling, or urge is petty or unjustified, or that you really have no effective response. Despite trying to talk yourself out of it, you feel the anger is still there. A good quick-and-easy next step is to short circuit your hostile thought, feeling, or urge by applying the strategy of thought stopping.

How to Use This Strategy

Thought stopping is simplicity itself. When you become aware of having a hostile attitude or thought, shout "at" it to "Stop!" If you're in the company of others—for example, listening to your surly teenager—you will want to make your "shout" a silent one, of course. On the other hand, if you're alone, perhaps listening to the latest outrage from a politician on the six o'clock news, go ahead and shout "Stop!"—at the top of your lungs, if you wish.

If saying "Stop!" doesn't work for you the first few times you try using it, vary your technique before you give up. To get you started, ask someone to help you. Establish a signal so that someone else cries "Stop!" when you start becoming riled. At first, your partner yells aloud at you to break your response to whatever is upsetting you. After you've mastered that over several nights or weeks, switch to shouting "Stop!" yourself. The next step will be when you can switch from your verbal to a silent "Stop!"

"I'm worried about Frank these days. . . .
It seems he just can't unwind."

You may want to keep in reserve one or more topics you enjoy thinking about—for example, a favorite person, hobby, or time of day. As soon as you get the "Stop!" signal, start thinking about the substitute. You can't concentrate at the same time on both that annoying politician on TV and the happy prospect of your next golf game.

In any situation, if the hostile thought, feeling, or urge remains after "Stop!" don't despair; many other strategies are available on your Hostility Roadmap.

Why This Strategy Works

Thought stopping is a cognitive behavior modification (just another term for changing thought) technique that has proved effective in helping people stop obsessive ruminations. You may be surprised how often this simple strategy is effective in helping you to rid yourself of hostile thoughts, feelings, or urges in those trivial, everyday situations that are the bane of so many of us hostile people. In one sense, thought stopping is an extension of the reason-with-yourself strategy, with your "rational self" (the angel on your shoulder) simply telling your less-than-rational "hostile self" (the devil on your other shoulder) to "cool it."

In his concept of "multimind," Robert Ornstein, a psychologist, adopts the perspective that our mind is not a single entity but rather a composite reflecting the evolutionary history of our species. Instead of a concept of the mind as composed of one self, the mind is viewed as a mosaic of inherited traits all coexisting within our heads.

According to the multimind perspective, most of our brain consists of ancient heritages, geared to survival in a very different world. As the first consideration is always survival, our consciousness gives priority to recent information, the unexpected or extraordinary, whether something looks better than other options, and how other people are behaving. Because of our biological inheritance, our big goals are keeping warm and safe, minding the body, and organizing our actions around the short-term contingencies of our environment.

To Ornstein, emotions are among the most important components of our mind. A mood or feeling can color an entire interchange, and feelings of anger will increase the likelihood that we will recall past angers. To apply Ornstein's model to this strategy, by yelling "Stop!" you remove the anger program from your consciousness. Your body can then stop preparations more appropriate for an attack from a predator or a one-time battle to establish rank order in the "tribe."

—————

The Strange Case of Dr. Jekyll and Mr. Hyde offers a literary example of multimind in action. In Robert Louis Stevenson's short novel, the doctor can at first control his experiment of unleashing his suppressed baser instincts. The personality and body of Edward

Hyde takes over only when Henry Jekyll drinks a chemical potion he mixes up in his laboratory. The indulgences Hyde allows are pleasurable to the repressed Jekyll, and eventually Hyde becomes "much exercised and nourished." In addition to utterly lacking a conscience and indulging all his appetites, Hyde centers every act and thought on self and gives free rein to his inordinate anger.

Henry Jekyll's experiments succeed; he proves that "man is not truly one, but truly two," in a vision prescient of Ornstein's multimind. ". . . I hazard to guess that man will be ultimately known for a mere polity of multifarious, incongruous and independent denizens."

In Stevenson's tale, Jekyll's self-indulgence of what he focuses his consciousness upon, with removal of all controls and conscience, eventually extracts a terrible price. Allowing his negative side expression eventually reinforces that kind of misbehavior.

> . . . I began to spy a danger that, if this were much prolonged, the balance of my nature might be permanently overthrown, the power of voluntary change be forfeited, and the character of Edward Hyde become irrevocably mine. . . . In the beginning, the difficulty had been to throw off the body of Jekyll, it had of late gradually but decidedly transferred itself to the other side. All things therefore seemed to point to this; that I was slowly losing hold of my original and better self, and becoming slowly incorporated with my second and worse.

Although the extreme example of Jekyll/Hyde is presented with literary license, the message shares some similarities to ours: When your baser instincts come to consciousness, tell them to "Stop!"

For all human beings a "Danger ahead!" message gets attention and becomes the focus of consciousness. The problem for us hostile people is that we perceive too many situations as dangerous. As a result, we are frequently preparing for fight or flight. By yelling "Stop!" you turn off the "Danger ahead!" message dominating you. With that stopped, you can refocus your consciousness on another topic of your choosing. This in turn will break the tight biological link between hostility and the fight-or-flight response.

Let's look at some examples of thought stopping in action.

Our daughter Jennifer is in her twenties and son Lloyd is in his late teens. Both are basically very good people, but as teenagers, like most people that age, they on occasion needed to reduce the stature of their parents to make growing up and leaving home easier. First Jennifer, followed several years later by Lloyd, disliked what we served for dinner, our requests for help with chores, family gatherings, and our driving.

Jennifer has now grown up, become a productive citizen, and is happily married. When she was breaking away, we found that the "Stop!" technique was an effective way to avoid overreacting to her criticisms. What was needed at the time was patience, not hostile responses. Sometimes we succeeded in applying the "Stop!" technique, and sometimes we didn't. Especially in retrospect, our patience was much more effective than snapping back at our daughter.

The "Stop!" technique continues to be useful on many occasions with Lloyd, who still lives at home. With the experience of Jennifer and our own increasing ability to stop hostility before it starts, we think that our batting average is improving. When we observe a mess in Lloyd's room, adapt to changes of plans, and react to what we perceive as insults, the "Stop!" technique keeps us from flying off the handle—at least a portion of the time!

This internal admonition to stop is a strategy our workshop participants tell us is particularly fun to use. They often substitute other statements for "Stop!" For example a conservative Republican found "There you go again!" very effective.

THE ABCS OF THOUGHT STOPPING

A. Decide if your anger does not merit your further attention, is unjustified, or you have no effective response.

B. Depending on the circumstances, silently, aloud, or by proxy yell "STOP!"

C. If the thought, feeling, or urge is now gone or less demanding of your attention, congratulate yourself on having successfully lowered your hostility; otherwise, move on to another strategy.

Exercises

1. Look over your Hostility Log and select some incidents you could have easily cut short at the beginning. Plan the next time you are in a similar situation to try your "Stop!" technique.

2. Following is a list of categories of people. You may react neutrally or positively to some of these groups, negatively to others. Make a note of any of these groups that have upset you in the past. Plan the next time you become annoyed at them either to take effective action or "Stop!" reacting.

- Men with long hair and earrings
- Men in military uniforms with short crewcuts
- Women with very short hair, wearing pants
- Women whose nipples show through their T-shirts
- People who sneer at women in revealing T-shirts
- Women with sprayed hair who wear polyester leisure suits and girdles
- Women with too much makeup and too much jewelry
- Teenagers who travel in large packs
- A busload of tourists in line at the restroom
- Any group in line at the restroom
- People who wear animal furs
- People who picket furriers
- People who giggle
- People who lack a sense of humor
- People who are too fat
- People who obviously don't eat enough to stay healthy
- People who chew gum in public
- People who pick their noses
- Parents who yell at their children in public places

- Public drunks

- People on drugs

- Prostitutes

- Salespersons who ignore you

- Salespersons who take care of the customer on the telephone while you cool your heels at the counter

- Kids who play their jam boxes at full volume in public settings

CHAPTER 5

Distract Yourself

One of Ten Canons of Conduct: "When angry count ten before you speak. If very angry a hundred."
Thomas Jefferson,
eighteenth- and nineteenth-century U.S. statesman

GENERAL PRINCIPLES

When to Use This Strategy

From now on, ask the three questions on your Hostility Roadmap every time you are in a situation that arouses hostile urges, feelings, or thoughts. When your appraisal leads to the conclusion that your ire is either petty or unjustified or that you have no effective response, simply distracting yourself, getting your mind off the anger, can often be effective.

How to Use This Strategy

Identify another focus in the situation, immersing yourself in it. To accomplish this, quickly look around to find something else to capture your attention. Choose the best new focus. When you become annoyed by the wait in the supermarket line, you can leaf through a magazine on sale adjacent to the checkout and save the price of the magazine, finishing it before you check out! Alternatively, just watch the people around you.

When frustrated in traffic, one of our workshop participants plays her favorite tape and sings along lustfully. You could also tune in to a talk-radio station, but beware you don't let yourself get riled anew by all the complaints hostile folks are calling in!

If nothing around you appeals, try daydreaming. Envision an ideal meal. Imagine yourself making love. Or being on a fantasy

vacation. You may be at the front of the line before your raft floats ashore on that South Pacific island!

Why This Strategy Works

Your consciousness has difficulty focusing on two subjects at once. When you start thinking about something new, you stop thinking about what is making you angry. By distracting your attention away, you short circuit the hostility cascade, with the result that the anger and stress hormones subside before harm is done.

Let's look at some examples. When Redford drives home from work, he keeps the daily newspaper on the front seat of the passenger side. When he comes to an intersection at rush hour that always takes a couple of stoplight cycles to get through, he scans the headlines of the newspaper while waiting for the light to change.

One workshop participant describes her job as generally enjoyable but with some unavoidable irritants she can't correct. Whenever she finds herself overwhelmed, yet without effective options for action, she retires to her office and closes the door. She then walks over to a large map of the United States on the wall. Closing her eyes, she lets her finger land randomly somewhere on the map. She then focuses her attention on that location. If she's ever traveled to that part of the country, she remembers past experiences there. If it's a place she's never been, she imagines what it's like. Once she feels calm again, she reopens the door and is ready to face the rest of her day.

We have a friend who repeats the same information endlessly and prefers not to be interrupted during his long soliloquies. If we remind him that he has already told us whatever he is talking about, he gets hurt. Because he prefers monologue to dialogue, "conversations" with him are excellent opportunities to plan menus, chapter outlines, and grant proposals. Although this is hardly an ideal arrangement or a basis for much real interaction, distracting our attention away from what he is saying does enable us to be reasonably polite without becoming as annoyed at him as we would otherwise be. (He does have redeeming features, and we want to keep his friendship.)

The potential benefits of the distraction strategy were demonstrated most dramatically in the *American Playhouse* production "Mrs. Cage," which aired on public television on May 20, 1992. As portrayed by Anne Bancroft, Mrs. Cage is an older woman who "loses it" in a supermarket parking lot during an attempted armed robbery.

Somehow she ends up with the robber's gun in her hand and shoots another shopper who stands screaming about her stolen purse while a box boy lies dying. Because Mrs. Cage appears to be a perfectly "normal" older woman, the policeman perplexedly asks what could have possessed her.

Mrs. Cage's reply: "She stood in the express lane with twenty-seven items. No coupons, she didn't have coupons. But she wrote a check. Grounds for murder, don't you think?"

If only Mrs. Cage had known about the distraction strategy and picked up a magazine instead!

THE ABCS OF DISTRACTING YOURSELF

A. After deciding that there's no effective way to change an anger-arousing situation, choose to distract yourself.

B. Take "time out" from the situation by devoting your attention to some less annoying focus—a magazine, radio program, people watching, or a fantasy.

C. If you succeed, reward yourself with a mental pat on the back. When the logjam breaks, get on with your real business. If distraction doesn't work, proceed to an additional strategy.

EXERCISES

1. Think of three distractions you might use in each of the following situations.

> **A.** You are at a public lecture but cannot hear the speaker because of a disruptive child in another section of the auditorium. You are becoming upset by this.

> **B.** You are driving to an airport and are forced to wait for a freight train to pass. You can feel a rising frustration.

> **C.** You are near the end of your lunch break, waiting in line at the post office. The elderly man at the window nearest you asks for five each of a long list of special stamps. Did you need this further hassle?

2. Look over your Hostility Log for situations in which distraction might have been effective. Consider some focuses you could have substituted.

CHAPTER 6

Meditate

"Blood is a very special kind of sap."
      Johann Wolfgang von Goethe,
        eighteenth- and nineteenth-century German author

Reprinted by permission of Tribune Media Services.

GENERAL PRINCIPLES

When to Use This Strategy

You've decided that a hostile thought, feeling, or urge of yours is either a waste of time, or unjustified, or there is no effective response available. You've tried reasoning with yourself. You've also tried the other, quicker and more simple deflection strategies (thought stopping and distraction), but to no avail. You are well aware that your pounding heart, quicker breathing, and shaky feelings are all indicators of the adrenaline that your adrenal gland is dumping into your bloodstream and of the potential harm it can do to your heart, arteries, and even immune system. The situation is beginning to get away from you, and more drastic action is in order.

This is a job for a simplified version of meditation. You don't want to run into a phone booth like Clark Kent and change into your Superman togs so you can fly off to smash your enemies. You're already changing into Superman—what's called for here is to run into the phone booth and change back into Clark Kent! Meditation will enable you to do just this: withdraw from the situation and go within and calm your mind to stop the cynical thoughts, thereby calming your body and blunting the adrenaline surge called forth by the anger.

How to Use This Strategy

In actual practice, the meditation strategy, although very powerful, is simple, deceptively so. The hard part is developing the skills that will enable you to grab hold of yourself even in the midst of a hostility-arousing situation.

As with any skill, your ability to meditate will be improved by regular practice. This means that you should practice when you are not in a "game situation." When the opposing fans are waving their hands and jumping up and down on the bleachers is not the optimum time to perfect your free-throw techniques. Instead, you practice in the quiet of the gym so that you can get every move down pat. Then, when the basketball game is on the line in the last seconds, you have so "burned" the moves into your body's memory you can swish the critical free throws even with the noise and distractions.

Your ability to meditate in stressful situations also increases with regular practice. Practice for fifteen minutes once a day in a quiet setting so that you can become adept at emptying your mind of all thought. Then, when you have been gratuitously insulted or held up by someone else's "incompetence," you will be better equipped to apply meditation skills on the spot to stop your cynical thoughts, quell your anger, and smother the aggressive urge. Here is what is involved:

1. Assume a comfortable position. No need to twist yourself into a pretzel; just sit in a chair, or cross-legged on the floor, or lie down.

2. Relax, as much as you can, all the muscles of your body. You may first want to try "progressive relaxation," in which you tense groups of muscles and then release them, beginning with your feet and toes and working your way up to your face.

3. Focus on your breathing. Notice when you breathe in and out. Pay close attention to the sensation of the passage of air across the membranes of your nose. Focus if you prefer on the air coming in or out of your chest or even belly. Let the air come to you. Exhale slowly, letting all the air out of your lungs. Try to breathe naturally, letting the air come in through your nostrils and out of your mouth.

4. Now begin every time you breathe out to repeat a word or phrase (mantra) that evokes the state you want to achieve—try "calm down" or "peace."

5. As you do this, you will probably notice seemingly random thoughts intruding upon your awareness. This is normal, so don't let it concern you. Simply return to paying attention to your breathing and saying the word or phrase with each exhalation. As you become more accomplished at meditation, you will find it easier to turn back intruding thoughts, and you will have fewer of them.

6. Continue to practice this breathing meditation for a set period of time—we recommend fifteen minutes a day. Take care to remove potential interruptions, such as telephone calls. If possible, don't schedule your practice after meals or before bedtime, as you want to be as alert as possible. The goal is to calm yourself, not to fall asleep.

If breathing does not work for you, try substituting visual concentration.

1. Focus on one image. This can be either something you imagine or something you actually see at that moment.

2. Try saying a word associated with the image as you breathe in and out. If your image is a tree, for instance, you might say "green."

If neither breathing nor a visual image succeeds, as a final possibility try focusing on a thought. For example, repeat several times a prayer or a poem that has meaning to you.

Daily practice in a serene setting will help to perfect your ability to meditate as a general skill. Next, you will want to try meditating in public every time you are forced to wait. This doesn't mean assuming the "yoga" position right there in the supermarket line! All that's needed is to start with a deep breath, then fix your eyes on a distant spot—say a clock on the wall—and then begin saying your mantra to yourself each time you breathe out. You will be standing there meditating in public, and no one but you will be aware of what you are doing.

You might begin with waits in your doctor's office, then work your way up to bank lines, followed by traffic jams. By then you will be rather proficient, so next try meditating when your spouse is late.

Finally, begin to meditate at the outset of every hostile thought, feeling, or urge that is petty or unjustified, or when you have no effective response. You might begin with the lying politician on television and eventually work your way up to meditating while your teenager cuts you down to size by attacking your appearance, habits, and personality.

Think of meditation as a quick way of taking, right then and there, a "time out" from situations that arouse your hostile thoughts, feelings, and actions.

Why This Strategy Works

By focusing on breathing and saying a relaxation-evoking word or phrase with each exhalation, you drive cynical thoughts from your mind. Although it takes extra effort on your part, meditation can be more effective than thought stopping or distraction in deflecting thoughts from cynical pathways.

Notice athletes at a foul line or at the top of a ski jump. Often they will take several deep breaths before beginning. In addition to providing a time delay, this practice reduces their physiological tension. As shown by some very sophisticated laboratory studies, meditation has a calming effect on fight-or-flight responses. Your breathing and heart rate slow down. Oxygen consumption decreases. Blood pressure is lowered or stabilized. There is a decrease of your skin's ability to conduct electric current, reflecting a reduction in sweating. Stress hormone levels in your blood actually fall. In addition, brain waves switch to a low arousal pattern, as can be measured with an electroencephalogram.

In some very real respects, practicing meditation is like taking a fast-acting tranquilizer right then and there. By shutting down your fight-or-flight responses on the spot, meditation can help you cut the biological cost that anger imposes on your heart, arteries, and immune system.

Don't be surprised if practicing meditation each day helps in more ways than just anger control. Meditators have been found to be more psychologically and physiologically stable and less anxious and to experience a sense of control in the world rather than one of being a passive victim. This may have to do with who takes up meditation, of course; meditators may be making other life-style changes that also affect their health. Nonetheless, all indications are that meditation is health enhancing to mind and body.

Beyond the biological benefits, a number of Eastern religions and societies claim that meditation imparts deep psychic benefits. Zen Buddhist priests, for example, practice breath meditation to gain religious insights.

Redford has been using various forms of meditation to relieve the stress or boredom of situations ever since he was a teenager. When he was an adolescent, he went to church every Sunday. Sometimes the sermon didn't engage his interest. Instead of fidgeting and getting upset, he used the "floaters"—the little specks inside the watery substance that fills the eyeball—in his right eye in a form of visual meditation. He would hold his right eye very still so that he could pick out one floater to focus on. Then he would position, with slight, very slow eye movements, that floater just above the head of the minister preaching the sermon. Then, ever so slowly and carefully, Redford would move his eye in such a way that the floater described a circle moving around the preacher's head. The object of the game was to see how many circles of the preacher's head he could make with the floater without touching the head or having the floater suddenly fly off into space—which it would certainly do with any sharp eye movement.

In this way, Redford was able to pass away five, ten, even fifteen minutes at a stretch without succumbing to the boredom that was the lot of other boys who didn't have "floater meditation" to fall back on.

Now that he is grown up and usually interested in the sermons at his church, Redford uses his meditation skills in other ways. Just as we have advised you to do, Redford will engage in brief meditation practices whenever he is detained in bank or supermarket lines, traffic, and the like. He has learned that meditating in these situations beats steaming at whoever is "responsible" for the slowdown.

Many of Redford's patients have been able to function more effectively by applying meditation and relaxation techniques in "real life" situations, although at first their hostile, Type A personalities made them resist. Two such patients were men who came to Redford's biofeedback clinic with the complaint of work-related headaches.

The first was an executive in charge of the payroll for a very large company. His lack of trust in others made it difficult for him to delegate any responsibility to those working under him in the payroll office. Consequently, he had to check every decision and its implementation. As each payroll deadline neared, his headaches grew more frequent and intense.

When Redford told him that he must take fifteen minutes every morning and afternoon and retreat to his office with the door closed and the phone off the hook and practice a meditation exercise, the executive replied, "You've got to be kidding. There are four thousand employees out there depending on me to see that the payroll gets out every two weeks!"

"Let's make a contract that you'll agree to try this for two weeks, and if it's interfering with your work I'll drop it," Redford replied. Not without some reluctance, the executive agreed to this trial period.

Two weeks later he was back in Redford's office for his return appointment. Somewhat sheepishly, he reported, "I've got to say I wouldn't have believed it. I've been doing the relaxation twice a day as we agreed. I haven't had a single headache, and you know something? I've been able to get my work done and leave the office thirty minutes early for the past week!" Somehow, even without his constant surveillance, the work had managed to get done.

The other patient was a scientist who worked for the Environmental Protection Agency. His headaches seemed to occur after long meetings he had to attend when the arguments grew acrimonious over what sanctions to impose on various businesses that had violated the EPA's regulations. He was particularly upset with some of his colleagues who he felt were far too lax in their enforcement.

When Redford gave him the assignment of surreptitiously practicing his meditation exercise *during* these lengthy meetings, he replied angrily, "What? And let those bastards get their way every time?" As with the "busy" executive, Redford was able to persuade the scientist to agree to a two-week trial period.

Two weeks later, the patient reported, "Well, I've got to hand it to you, Doc—the headaches are much better. And"—here his face blossomed into a broad grin—"I've been winning twice as many points in those damned meetings! Somehow, I seem to be able to think better since I've been taking those little 'time outs' you suggested."

Both these men had resisted the idea of taking time out of their work to meditate because their hostility caused them to fear that they would lose control: The payroll wouldn't get out, the argument would be lost. But their fears were not confirmed. Instead, by taking time to reduce their flight-or-flight system's response to the work situation, they were able not only to get rid of their troublesome headaches but also to function more effectively in their jobs.

It was important that they commit to practicing their relaxation at work for at least two weeks. Redford's experience in treating headache patients had taught him that it took this long for a patient with headaches to begin to realize the benefits of relaxation. Therefore he could predict that if they really stuck with it that long they would be back with the reports of improvement.

Similar reasoning led us earlier to encourage you to commit yourself to a four-week trial of keeping your Hostility Log and using the Hostility Roadmap to guide you to the hostility- and anger-control strategies you are learning about in this book. These strategies are no magical overnight cure for your hostile ways; but if you will give them an honest try for four weeks the way Redford's headache patients did, we predict that you will be so encouraged by your progress that it will be easier to continue.

THE ABCS OF MEDITATION

A. Relax, focusing your total attention on breathing naturally.

B. Repeat a calming word or phrase every time you breathe out.

C. Continue until the crisis has passed. Whenever your concentration wanders, simply return the focus to your breathing.

EXERCISES

1. As long as you are developing your survival skills, meditate for a set period of time each day.

2. If meditation turns out to be an effective strategy for you, we recommend that you read an excellent book by Jon Kabat-Zinn, *Full Catastrophe Living* (New York: Delacorte, 1990). With careful and detailed instruction, Dr. Kabat-Zinn teaches meditation skills as a means to develop moment-by-moment awareness of the self and the body. The meditator thus develops a sense of wholeness. Kabat-Zinn reports that after becoming proficient meditators, his patients are then able to face stress, pain, and illness with equanimity and often even triumph over their problems.

CHAPTER 7

Avoid Overstimulation

"Exercise and temperance can preserve something of our early vigor even into old age."

Cicero,

first-century B.C. Roman statesman

GENERAL PRINCIPLES

When to Use This Strategy

Hostile people should be especially careful to treat their bodies well, as remaining composed is easier with a calm nervous system. To help achieve this nonagitated state, give up or cut back on nicotine, caffeine, and sweets as much as you can. In addition, exercise regularly.

Any student of biology can show you through dozens of simple experiments that what a body ingests affects its functioning. Any medical student can likewise demonstrate that the brain, other nerves, and the cardiovascular system of human beings can be greatly affected by certain chemicals.

Some substances are by nature stimulants to the nervous and cardiovascular systems. Nicotine, caffeine (present in coffee, tea, caffeinated sodas, chocolate, some over-the-counter drugs), and to a lesser extent sugar are the three most frequently used stimulants in our culture. The state of overstimulation they induce usually is temporary, followed by a flattening of responsiveness. This pattern is repeated each time the substance is ingested.

As you already know, hostile personalities possess nervous systems that react too easily, even without stimulants. Nicotine, caffeine, and to a lesser extent sugar can exacerbate this hyperreactivity. The nervous system is further stimulated when what is needed is to dampen responsiveness.

Even more important, hostile persons lack the ability to turn off their reactions by using their parasympathetic nervous system to calm back down soon. Instead they remain highly stimulated. When a hostile person has previously ingested nicotine, caffeine, or sugar, calming down will be even more difficult than usual. Therefore, the ingestion of these stimulants can add more stress and strain to an already overtaxed body.

Exercise has the opposite effect.

How to Use This Strategy

Helping you to give up nicotine, caffeine, and sweets is only an indirect goal of this book. Each of these endeavors is a major project that requires special commitment, probably repeated attempts, and maybe professional help.

As Redford reported in chapter 2, hostile persons have great difficulty giving up these stimulants, *yet they are very susceptible to the harmful effects of these substances.* The less the dependence on nicotine, caffeine, and sugar, the greater the chances of conquering hostility.

Equally valid is to turn around the perspective on the hostility/substance-dependence combination. The less you react with hostility to day-to-day occurrences in your life, the less you may need relaxants and stimulants.

Starting an exercise program is relatively easy for some individuals and likely to alleviate both substance overindulgence and hostility. If you are over forty or if you suspect or know that you have cardiovascular disease already, be sure to have a physical checkup before you begin an exercise program. Aim for sustained mildly aerobic activity several times a week. Recommended heartbeat rates differ according to age, so you need to find out your target rate and to monitor your heartbeat periodically during exercise to be certain that you are within safe limits.

Sustained relatively mild exercise like swimming, light jogging, riding a bicycle, or even vigorous walking will elevate your heartbeat, which you should keep elevated for at least twenty minutes. Less salutary are "stop and go" sports, like tennis, baseball, or pitching horseshoes.

Avoid becoming too competitive or adopting an attitude of always trying to improve your performance. You are exercising to calm your nervous system, not to extend overachievement to yet another area of your life.

Give some thought to what sports you most like. Experiment, without making any initial investment or commitment. Your emphasis should be on enjoying yourself, not focusing on exercise as healthful.

Forgive yourself when you can't exercise, but go back to regular participation as soon as you can.

Why This Strategy Works

Many Americans attempt to regulate their psychic states with substances. They consume nicotine, caffeine, and sugar in the early morning for alertness and energy and to recover from the relaxants of the previous evening. Once their bodies become overstimulated by either what has been ingested or a hostile incident, they repeat the pattern by ingesting alcohol and too much food in an attempt to calm down. As Redford noted in chapter 2, hostile people are more likely than others to use all of these substances.

Each day, many Americans repeat this destructive pattern of overstimulation and attempts to calm down, despite its ineffectiveness and its damaging effects on both relationships and health. Gradually, these habits become increasingly harmful, with ever-larger quantities of stimulants and relaxants ingested, perhaps in an attempt to curb ever more frequent outbursts of hostility. Once a person breaks this pattern, diminishing both hostility and substance dependence should become easier.

Virginia gave up cigarettes and caffeine years ago, exercises four times a week, and usually watches her calories and cholesterol. She drinks wine and beer mainly at social gatherings only. All of this is rather easy for her, for reasons both of temperament and relatively modest appetites.

Redford has approached life more lustfully. In his thirties, he could tell you where in Dallas to get a fifty-two-ounce porterhouse steak! On occasion, usually at national conferences, he and some drinking buddies used to consume great quantities of alcohol, and each evening he was home, he had a couple of beers or glasses of wine. He has always smoked an occasional pipe and drunk a moderate amount of coffee in the morning. He took up tennis several years ago and played sporadically.

Over the years, Redford looked forward more and more to his drink when he got home and continued to live the indulgent life at national conferences. His weight began to creep up, and his formerly athletic muscle tone weakened. A few years after his increased girth became noticeable, he learned that one of his good friends and drinking buddies was an alcoholic. This finally got Redford's attention, and he began to reconsider his personal habits.

In reaction, Redford bought a fancy new tennis racket. He lined up a number of tennis partners so he could always count on at least one of them being available. During weekdays, he switched to nonalcoholic beer. To relax in the evenings now, instead of having the usual two glasses of wine, he soaks a long while in a hot bath while he reads the newspaper.

How much of Redford's progress in hostility control is related to his new moderation, he cannot say. Certainly all of his new habits fit together congenially. Virginia feels that he is more alert and invested in her than when he was having a couple of drinks before dinner. For her, evenings are a lot more enjoyable than before, which makes her easier to live with.

THE ABCS OF AVOIDING OVERSTIMULATION

A. Make it your goal to cut back as much as you can or to eliminate nicotine, caffeine, and sweets. This can be either a direct goal or you can first try to achieve it indirectly through hostility control.

B. Set as another goal exercising several times a week.

C. Congratulate yourself when you achieve these goals; accept that it is common to fail, and when you do, simply begin anew.

EXERCISES

1. Consider your substance habits. If you heavily use any of the stimulants or relaxants mentioned, record for a week or so in your Hostility Log those occasions when you indulge. See if you can note any correlation between your cynicism/anger/aggression and substance ingestions. (If you are trying to give up a habit, you may be temporarily more irritable, but that will diminish eventually.)

2. Likewise, record in your Hostility Log when you exercise so that you can determine if this correlates with hostility.

A STRATEGY TO HELP YOU
ACT EFFECTIVELY

You are learning anger control as a means of improving your mental and physical health. This does *not* mean that you are never going to have angry feelings, nor that you shouldn't act on them.

Sometimes you will answer the questions on your Hostility Roadmap with "yes." In other words, in these instances the matter is *not* trivial. Your cynical thoughts and anger *are* justified. And you do have reasonable responses. In these circumstances, you certainly should take action. The challenge, however, is to take action effectively without lashing out, sabotaging your efforts through anger, or otherwise losing your cool. The next chapter explains how.

CHAPTER **8**

Assert Yourself

"Anyone can become angry—that is easy, but to be angry with the right person, to the right degree, at the right time, for the right purpose, and in the right way—this is not easy."

> Aristotle,
> fourth-century B.C. Greek philosopher

Reprinted with permission of Universal Press Syndicate.

GENERAL PRINCIPLES

When to Use This Strategy

Sometimes you can decide, on a purely rational, objective basis, that hostility is not only justified but, further, that you should act to correct the injustice. Without consulting you, your spouse writes a big check on your joint account for a new car when you wanted to save money toward the down payment for a house. You and a colleague have jointly prepared a special report; now he is presenting the findings without acknowledging your contributions.

Controlling your anger does not mean ignoring injustices to others, either. Righteous indignation on behalf of others has a long and proud history. Many Jewish prophets—Isaiah and Amos come first to mind—proclaimed Yahweh's wrath against wayward peoples. Jesus angrily threw the money changers from the temple. Civil rights leaders such as Martin Luther King, Jr., preached brotherly love and stood their ground against threats and actions as they broke unjust laws, year after year.

By allowing yourself a range of strategies—both asserting and deflecting options—you can balance your twin goals of preventing petty matters from riling you and remaining focused on your legitimate rights and those of others. Sometimes you may choose to take a stand for what is right; at other times you may prefer to tune out the situation. Real injustices *do* exist in the world. The goal in learning to control your hostility is not to become insensitive to all injustices but rather to become more focused and selective.

Unlike meditation, in which you withdraw, assertion will project you into the situation. Assertion, as opposed to aggression, involves asking others to change a specific behavior. You limit your request, however embellished, to that specific focus. Also, you deliver your request calmly and respectfully.

How to Use This Strategy

First decide, via reasoning through the Hostility Roadmap, if it is worth the effort to try to get the perpetrator to change. Next decide if you or someone you wish to protect is being truly mistreated. If you have answered yes to both, proceed to evaluate whether you have potentially effective options. If the perpetrator is someone who cut you off in traffic and then exited the freeway, for instance, there is little you can really do. If, on the other hand, the offending party is a co-worker who always interrupts you before you finish your sentences, you might very well decide that you do have an effective response. When all of your answers to Roadmap questions are positive, you need the strategy of assertion.

In face-to-face contacts, remember that *much or most of your message will be nonverbal:* the way you stand, the expression on your face, and so on. Therefore, it is extremely important that you be perceived as being nonhostile yourself. Your goal is to be heard, not to cause the other party to tune you out.

Therefore, deliver your remarks in a respectful tone of voice and try to avoid speaking too loudly or rapidly. As Redford's colleague John Barefoot has shown, nonverbal communications—frowns, sneers, derisive tones of voice, and the like—convey the most reliable information about someone's true hostility level. Even the most politely worded request, delivered by someone with a scowl, won't command the listener's respectful attention. Adopt a manner dignified and hopeful, with appropriate facial expression and hand gestures. Appear as relaxed as you can manage! If you are to succeed in controlling the situation, you need to appear in control of yourself.

If you are communicating in writing instead of in person, make your prose carefully reasoned and respectful.

You will, in addition, want to tailor your response to the situation. Study the different types of assertion listed here, as you will need all of them in your repertoire. Each one builds upon the preceding ones. You may not need to bring out "the big gun" in each situation, but in general, the more complex your response, the more of these techniques you will probably have to use.

MAKE A SIMPLE ASSERTION

Sometimes a short request is all that's needed. You state what you want and let that suffice. "Excuse me, please let me finish what I am saying."

DESCRIBE THE MISBEHAVIOR

If appropriate, you may want to preface your request with an explicit description of what you perceive to be the misbehavior of the other person. Always be very *specific* about what *overt behavior you want changed.* "You are eating most of the cashews before I get a chance to have any; please wait until I can share them with you" is a lot easier to comply with than the injunction "Would you please try to be more considerate?"

Avoid categorical statements like "You always" or "You never." Use statements like "Just now, when you did x." Because you will often be upset by the unpleasant feelings you are experiencing in these situations, it can be helpful if you do a quick meditation—or even just take a few slow, deep breaths—before you speak.

A calmer voice is more likely to elicit a similar response than a voice clearly charged with emotion.

EMPATHIZE

If your request might offend the other person, preface it with an understanding of his or her point of view. "The sign is hard to see beneath the oil slicks, but where you are about to park is reserved for the handicapped only." (The behavior you request in this example is implied, but clear.)

REMIND THE OTHER PERSON OF A PROMISE

If you're upset because someone broke a promise to you, first remind the person what was promised. Then objectively describe what the person actually did. Conclude by stating what you want. We are still dealing with minor situations, where only a simple response is appropriate.

"Mary, you and I agreed that you would let me know about all the calls I received.

"Mr. Jones tells me he left a message with you the other day, yet I never heard about his call. As a result, I missed hearing about a conference.

"I want you always to let me know about every call I get. Is that something you can do in the future?"

SHARE YOUR FEELINGS

Describe to the other person the feelings you experienced as a result of the behavior you just described. Don't be reticent. You are the world's expert on the feelings you experience in any situation, and they are authentic. No one can deny your feelings, even if he or she disputes the facts of the situation. In describing your feelings, be sure to speak in personal terms. Say, "I feel disappointed" rather than "This situation is disappointing." At the same time, tell the other person that you experience these feelings as unpleasant.

Now, ask the other person to help you eliminate these unpleasant feelings by changing—in very specific ways—his or her behavior that stimulated the feelings. You might want to preface this request when appropriate by reassuring the other person that you really do value him or her. For example, "I really like going out with you. But when you disappoint me by not showing up, I am out of sorts for the rest of the day. I need for you to be punctual the next time we have a date."

STATE THE CONSEQUENCES

The last optional step is to inform the other person what the consequences will be if he or she is unable to change. Let us assume that you have informed a driver that the parking place she has taken is reserved for the disabled and the driver has not moved her car. You might next say, "If you stay in the disabled spot, I'll contact the security guards." (This assumes you are confident that this situation won't pose a danger.)

Consequences can range from relatively minor ones, such as "If you can't stop giving me instructions while I am trying to cook dinner, you'll either have to stay out of the kitchen or cook dinner yourself," to clearly major ones: "If you are unable to stop criticizing my competence in doing everything, from driving, to cooking, to being on the house-and-grounds committee at church, I may have to leave you." You must *limit yourself to consequences you are willing to follow through on,* so *think carefully before issuing any ultimatums.*

ADDITIONAL GUIDELINES

After you finish and it's the other person's turn to speak, give him or her your respectful, undivided attention. After each of you has had as many turns as you need, a compromise may be what's most appropriate, with each of you getting part of what's requested. A sample dialogue follows.

"I hear you saying that it's important to you that I show up on time. But sometimes I don't know how long my meetings will run."

"That leaves me feeling stood up, disappointed, and upset."

"But I can't control at what hour those special meetings break up."

"What days are they held?"

"On Tuesdays, Thursdays, and Saturdays."

"Suppose I rearrange my schedule to meet you on Mondays, Wednesdays, and Fridays. Could you then agree to be on time?"

In addition to specific incidents that set you off, you may become angry because of mistreatment based on your race, gender, age, sexual orientation, social class, or ethnic group. Such insults can be a spur to legitimate anger. Here, you may want to keep some additional guidelines in mind as you focus on taking effective action.

In *The Dance of Anger,* a guide to changing the patterns of intimate relationships, Harriet Lerner, a family psychotherapist, sees women's anger as potentially a signal that can preserve the integrity of self. The advice she offers to women who feel discriminated against is good advice for all of us who experience discrimination.

- If you are angry for a [good] reason, your anger always deserves your respect and attention.

- Express what you want instead of venting your spleen. Your goals should be clear first of all to yourself. This means you must know "Who am I? What do I want? What do I deserve?"

- If you are angry with someone, *that's* the person you should tell.

- If you want to go up the hierarchy with your anger, go through appropriate channels openly.

- Avoid secrets.

Let's illustrate with an example from the workplace. Your boss gives all the juicy assignments to someone else in your department. On all previous assignments, you have turned in reports that she has declared at least satisfactory and sometimes excellent. You feel ready for bigger challenges and have told her that. Still, you get all the dinky assignments while the other person gets a chance to shine.

Don't complain to your co-workers. Instead, first complain to your boss. If she doesn't address your concerns, complain again. Let your boss know that you will seek redress by speaking to

someone higher up in the company, if you aren't given better assignments. If you aren't, follow through.

When you practice assertion, usually you are requesting something from others. Most people will respond positively to your
respectful attempt to interact with them in an assertive way on some
specific issue. Occasionally, no matter how well you practice the
assertion strategy, the other person will be unable or unwilling to
change. Because ultimately no matter how skillful you are, you
cannot control others, sometimes you won't get what you want.

After such a failure, consider the options anew. The situation
may have merited one try on your part, but if the stakes are really
comparatively small, you always have the option of dropping the
matter after your initial attempt has failed. You can simply forgive
the person (chapter 15) or perhaps go on to some fallback strategies
for deflecting hostility (chapters 4, 5, and 6).

On the other hand, if the stakes are large, you may want to
persevere. Remember that you can always escalate your level of
assertion. A simple request can become next time an empathizing
request, which can become the third time a request in which you
share your feelings, which can be followed by reminding others of
the consequences of their behavior.

In chapter 20, we will discuss in more detail options for dealing with the special case of a hostile partner.

Why This Strategy Works

Harsh words and gestures nearly always elicit similar behavior
directed back toward you. In practicing assertion, you concentrate
on what you need and want, not on what may further rile the other
person and you.

Assertion quickly switches you out of a physiological response
of anticipated danger to more goal-oriented behaviors.

———

Virginia defends quite effectively the rights of others, including people she has never met. She's no pushover at work, either, nor
is she too meek a friend. But when someone she admires very much
or a family member tries to control her behavior, they often succeed. Now that she has practiced her assertion skills, her track
record is much better. Here are some examples of her assertion
techniques that work with Redford.

- "Your driving suggestions are not helpful." (Time 1)
  "I request you not make driving suggestions." (Time 2)
  "If you want us to ride together, you must stop making driving suggestions." (Time 3)

- "I prefer to cook the spaghetti without help."

- "Should we always take the bigger slice ourselves or offer that to each other?"

- "Let's each be first writer for half the chapters. What are your first preferences?"

- "I want my half of the bottle of wine, without having to chug-a-lug."

- "You know we need to get a draft of the book off soon. When this weekend do you prefer we discuss our next steps?"

Assertion skills have also come in handy for Redford as he has had to interact with new faculty colleagues who have moved to Duke from "up north." On many occasions Redford has experienced the "New York" style of argument as a personal attack on him rather than just a usual mode of relating.

After feeling hurt and put down when new colleagues—who may have been old friends of his even before coming to Duke—told him yet again that a suggestion he had made is "simply ridiculous," Redford finally decided on one occasion it was time to do something.

His first impulse was to respond in kind, perhaps to say, "Well, I think your proposal stinks!" Given Redford's southern background, however, this would have been an aggressive, rather than an assertive approach. Luckily, Redford was able to keep his emotions in check and practice what we are preaching here.

"I really do value your input on this," he told his colleague, "and I know you really want to be helpful."

"However," Redford continued, "when you tell me my ideas are 'ridiculous,' I feel like some kind of incompetent who can't even present his thoughts coherently. I don't particularly like feeling this way, especially when interacting with a good friend and respected colleague like you."

"Therefore, I hope that when in the future you think that some suggestion I am presenting is less than clear, you'll simply ask me to clarify it, rather than use language like 'That's ridiculous!' If you can do that, I won't get my feelings so hurt, and we'll be more likely to figure out the best course of action, not to mention keep our friendship going the way we'd both like. Whaddya say?"

Of course, Redford could have realized right away that his friend's comments reflected only a difference of style, not of substance. Then he could have practiced tolerance, as we suggest in chapter 14.

THE ABCS OF ASSERTION

A. Determine that the situation seems important to you, that you or some other persons you wish to defend have genuinely been mistreated, and that some potentially effective actions are available.

B. Decide how much of an initial assertion is called for:

> You can make a simple request;
>> plus
> You can describe the misbehavior;
>> plus
> You can empathize with the other person;
>> plus
> You can remind the other person about earlier promises;
>> plus
> You can add information about your own feelings;
>> plus
> You can state the consequences of further misbehavior.

C. Observe the outcome. If your request has been granted, or if you have reached a successful compromise, congratulate yourself and thank the other person for complying. If no such resolution was possible and you have already carried through on all the consequences you promised to deliver if the matter wasn't resolved, you need to consider a new round of options.

> You can drop the matter, forgiving the other person and going back to deflection strategies if necessary.
>> or
> You can repeat and/or escalate your assertion.

EXERCISES

1. Imagine how you would respond assertively to each of the following situations.

A. You are giving a report, and the same person interrupts you for the third time with a sidetracking question.

B. Someone breaks into the restroom line when you are already feeling uncomfortable.

C. Your child "forgets" to give you a note from his teacher about missing homework.

D. Despite your request yesterday, your child still has not picked up the mess in her bedroom.

E. The appliance-repair service does not want to give you an exact time when they'll be at your house.

F. You learn that your child's school is receiving only half as large athletic allocations as more prosperous districts in the same school system.

G. You become horrified, angry, and ashamed by the following health-care comparisons between children in the United States and western European nations.

- Childhood mortality rates are higher in the United States than in Europe at all age levels, most markedly among one- to four-year-olds and fifteen- to nineteen-year-olds.

- Immunization rates for U.S. preschoolers are lower than in Europe.

- U.S. children are less likely to have a regular source of medical care than are their European counterparts.

- U.S. children are far more likely than children in Europe to experience injury-related deaths.

2. Pick some examples from your Hostility Log in which you became angry with another person because of how he or she was treating you. Carefully outline how you would respond with assertion.

STRATEGIES TO HELP YOU IMPROVE RELATIONSHIPS

Is it the misbehavior of others that usually upsets you? Look over your Hostility Log with this question in mind. Chances are, this more than anything else is responsible for most of your entries.

The goal of the next eight chapters is to improve your relationships with others. Success at this important task should reduce your number of hostile encounters, which in turn will reduce stress and strain on your mind and body.

When you set out looking for misbehavior in others, you will very likely find—even cause—it. Train yourself, instead, to be less eternally vigilant ("Practice Trusting Others," chapter 11). Under certain circumstances, you need also to learn how to forgive people who actually have mistreated you (chapter 15).

Tune others out and you are left with only your own perspective. On the other hand, you can learn to build bridges of positive understanding. You can learn to be a better listener (chapter 10), more sensitive to the thoughts and feelings of others (chapter 13), and more tolerant (chapter 14). These strategies will help reduce the frequency and intensity of entries in your Hostility Log.

With practice, you can learn to care about and for others. The chapters on pets (9), community service (12), and confidants (16) will show you how.

All of these strategies should help you get beyond that exclusive focus on yourself—*your* interests, feelings, needs, and perspective. As your ability to focus on others grows, so will their ability—and inclination—to focus on you. At that point, other people become not a source so much of irritation as one of mutual enjoyment and enrichment. You will replace health-damaging isolation with the health-enhancing benefits of social support and connectedness.

CHAPTER 9

Care for a Pet

"I think I could turn and live with animals, they are so placid and self-contained."   Walt Whitman,
                                          nineteenth-century U.S. poet

"Who's my best friend?"

© 1991 William Steig

GENERAL PRINCIPLES

When to Use This Strategy

If you can see that your hostility is alienating you from other people, or if you can appreciate that at least a portion of the isolation you feel grows out of your cynical expectations that others will behave badly, then the experience of owning and caring for a pet may offer you a path out of the isolation into which hostility has fenced you.

Owners usually value their pets. A large series of surveys have shown that in the United States from 48 to 80 percent of owners describe their pets as members of the family. Dog owners spend on the average 150 minutes a day with their dogs; cat owners, 86

**"Hold it right there, Doreen! ... Leave if you must —
but the dog *stays*!"**

minutes. At the same time, the demands of pets are limited. If you have the appropriate temperament and inclination, pet ownership can provide you with a safe and nonthreatening opportunity to learn how to be an active participant in a trusting, caring relationship that will make few demands of you.

How to Use This Strategy

The first step is to choose what kind of pet. Not surprising, the more demonstrative species require more care from you.

Dogs are affectionate, welcoming, intelligent, and obedient. They also require your active involvement in their daily care. They must be let out or walked at least twice a day, and they must be fed at a specific time each day. You must, of course, follow this regimen seven days a week. If you want to go away for the weekend, you cannot leave the dog home alone—you must either take it with you, board it, or arrange for someone to walk and feed it at your home. Nonetheless, the rewards offered by the companionship of a dog outweigh these inconveniences, at least for millions the world over.

Cats require far less constant care and adapt well to life in small apartments. They use a litter box, so you don't have to let them outside, and their eating habits are different. Unlike dogs, who will eat all the food before them every time, cats can nibble along on a bowl of dry food for several days. Consequently, you can leave a cat alone when you want to take off on the spur of the moment for a long weekend. Like dogs, cats can be very loving and loyal, but they also have an independent streak. It is *you* who owns the dog, but with felines it often seems as if *the cat* is the boss and you are the one who is owned. As the millions of cat books sold every year attest, this is not a problem for those who are comfortable with this kind of relationship.

Other sorts of pets—fish, for example—may require less care and can provide some of the rewards of pet ownership. But with a dog or cat you will have more interaction. We have owned both dogs and cats, and both are well worth the effort—for us, that is, but not necessarily for everyone. One busy doctor and lawyer we know in San Francisco have kept a series of dearly loved guinea pigs throughout their thirty-year-long marriage. For them, a guinea pig is the ideal pet.

You may find it helpful to check out books on dogs, cats, birds, rodents, fish, or whatever other animal you think might appeal to you to learn more about the characteristics of specific species and breeds.

Once you have decided on the type of pet, proceed cautiously! A low-risk way to try the pet strategy is to take care of a friend's pet for a weekend. We highly recommend such a trial, as some of our workshop participants report themselves more hassled than calmed by pet ownership.

The last time we acquired a dog, we reduced the hassles of pet ownership by acquiring our pet already fully grown and housebroken. By contacting the local kennel club from a listing in the classifieds, we eventually located a veterinarian who raises whippets for the show ring but waits until the dogs are fully grown to finish culling the litter. Lolly had already received all her shots and the best of care in other ways as well. Also, because she was trained to submit to the indignities of grooming, she was patient with our then-young children. Our purchase price was reasonable, because the previous owner wanted to be sure Lolly had a good home and most potential buyers looking for a family pet preferred a puppy. We avoided the hassles of housebreaking and possible puppy tooth-marks on our furniture yet still got a wonderful pet.

Why This Strategy Works

Pets make very few demands on you, other than food and care. At the same time, they provide unquestioning devotion. When Ubiquity, our first cat, was part of our family, she often cuddled up to Redford and gave his arm the most pleasurable baths with her rough yet gentle tongue. She demanded so little in return! This helped him to convince himself that surely there must also be many humans with whom you can also get along with that well, albeit in more complex ways.

Because pets are of simpler intelligence and emotional consti-tution than humans, the rational part of our brain finds it easier to know that they do not act out of the ulterior, selfish motives we so often see behind the behavior of fellow humans.

Taking care of a pet is good practice when it comes to taking better care of your fellow humans as well.

Pet ownership involves physical contact. If you choose a mam-mal, you will touch your pet and be touched by it. This is in itself comforting, as well as good practice in relating to others physically. Also, contact with an animal helps reestablish the bond of human beings with the natural world, a bond we have allowed to weaken in this modern age.

Besides all these logical reasons, several research studies sug-gest that both the physical and emotional well-being of pet owners are better than that of the rest of the population. In his book *The Language of the Heart,* James Lynch reports on three physiological studies demonstrating the health benefits of pet companionship. One of these studies is of patients from the coronary care unit at the University of Maryland Hospital. At the time of hospitalization, all of the subjects had experienced a heart attack or currently had severe angina. In the one-year follow-up period, 28 percent of the patients who did not own pets had died, compared with only 6 percent of pet owners. Of course part of this effect might reflect who felt well enough to own a pet. Yet even when general physical health and extent of cardiovascular disease were controlled for, pet ownership remained an independent predictor of survival.

In another study by Lynch, thirty-six children between the ages of nine and sixteen had their blood pressure recorded when reading and at rest. Blood pressure always rose when they were reading, but less so in the presence of a friendly, previously unknown dog. This calming effect was especially pronounced if the dog had been present from the beginning.

In a study of people and their pets in the waiting room at the University of Pennsylvania Veterinary Clinic, experimenters measured the pet owners' blood pressure. When the pet owners talked with the experimenter, their blood pressure rose. In contrast, when pet owners talked to their pets, their blood pressure either did not change or actually decreased.

Nursing homes around the country have discovered that encouraging older people to love and care for pets raises people's spirits.

Animals also appear to benefit from positive human contact. A dog's heart rate slows down in the extended presence of humans, especially if the person pets the animal. The flow of blood in the dog's coronary arteries increases when a person enters the room. The presence of comforting humans can partly ameliorate the effects of electric shock on a dog's cardiovascular system. Not only is your pet improving your health, but your presence benefits your pet as well.

Buck, the great dog described by Jack London in *The Call of the Wild,* is one of the bravest and most loyal characters in literature. John Thornton saves Buck's life, and Buck becomes his dog after that. The deep bond between them is severed only when Thornton dies.

> This man had saved his life, which was something; but, further, he was the ideal master. Other men saw to the welfare of their dogs from a sense of duty and business expediency; he saw to the welfare of his as if they were his own children, because he could not help it. And he saw further. He never forgot a kindly greeting or a cheering word, and to sit down for a long talk with them

("gas" he called it) was as much his delight as theirs. He had a way of taking Buck's head roughly between his hands, and resting his own head upon Buck's, of shaking him back and forth, the while calling him ill names that to Buck were love names. Buck knew no greater joy than that rough embrace and the sound of murmured oaths, and at each jerk back and forth it seemed that his heart would be shaken out of his body so great was its ecstasy. And when, released, he sprang to his feet, his mouth laughing, his eyes eloquent, his throat vibrant with unuttered sound, and in that fashion remained without movement, John Thornton would reverently exclaim, "God! you can all but speak!"

Buck had a trick of love expression that was akin to hurt. He would often seize Thornton's hand in his mouth and close so fiercely that the flesh bore the impress of his teeth for some time afterward. And as Buck understood the oaths to be love words, so the man understood this feigned bite for a caress.

For the most part, however, Buck's love was expressed in adoration. While he went wild with happiness when Thornton touched him or spoke to him, he did not seek these tokens. . . . He would lie by the hour, eager, alert, at Thornton's feet, looking up into his face, dwelling upon it, studying it, following with keenest interest each fleeting expression, every movement or change of feature. Or, as chance might have it, he would lie farther away, to the side or rear, watching the outlines of the man and the occasional movements of his body. And often, such was the communion in which they lived, the strength of Buck's gaze would draw John Thornton's head around, and he would return the gaze, without speech, his heart shining out of his eyes as Buck's heart shone out.

What a friend *both* Buck and John Thornton had!

THE ABCS OF CARING FOR A PET

A. Decide that your loneliness and isolation from other people might be alleviated if you had the companionship of a pet.

B. Consider carefully the time and energy you will be able to invest. Research the characteristics of various breeds and borrow for the weekend a pet of the type you are considering. If that goes well, acquire your pet.

C. Make your pet a friend. Accept its undemanding devotion as the blessing it is. Try to return to it the same loving care. Be patient and reap the rewards. You will find your ability to do likewise with humans increasing as well.

EXERCISES

1. If you already own a pet, try to get better acquainted with it.

2. If you do not own a pet but are interested in considering the possibility, borrow from the public library several appropriate books. For example, Gino Pugnett's *Dogs* (New York: Simon and Schuster, 1980), which is available in paperback, will give you a picture and description of 324 breeds.

3. For inspiration as well as information about what makes an owner fond of a cat or dog, read literary works featuring these species. John Steinbeck vividly portrays his close relationship with his dog in *Travels with Charley in Search of America.* In a collection of poems entitled *Old Possum's Book of Practical Cats,* T. S. Eliot prefers to admire cats from a greater distance.

CHAPTER **10**

Listen!

"The reason why we have two ears and only one mouth is that we may listen the more and talk the less."
Zeno,
fifth-century B.C. Greek philosopher

CALVIN AND HOBBES copyright 1986. Distributed by Universal Press Syndicate. Reprinted with permission. All rights reserved.

GENERAL PRINCIPLES

When to Use This Strategy

Use the *listen!* strategy frequently to learn to orient yourself toward others. Most hostile people are very *self-involved,* an understandable complement to their cynicism. The longstanding focus on self, as well as the need to be in control, grows out of a lack of trust in others. If you don't place much trust in other people, you have only yourself to count on. Hence, much of your conversation is laced with references to yourself—*I, me, mine.* This low level of trust in others and its attendant high level of self-involvement frequently cause the hostile person to pay little attention to what the other person is saying or doing.

Rather than trying to hear and understand, do you find yourself instead busily concentrating on your own thoughts, forming

118

"Brad, we've got to talk."

your own agenda about what to say next? This is why conversations with hostile people can be so frustrating—concerned mainly with their own ideas rather than trying to learn from others, they often interrupt before the other person has even had a chance to complete a sentence. Even if the hostile listener can anticipate what is said, the speaker is probably still insulted. As the columnist George F. Will once said when his fellow commentator William F. Buckley tried to finish a sentence for him, "Bill, I am the world's expert on how I want to end my sentence!"

Even when one's response relates to what the other person says, it very often serves mainly to shift the focus back to oneself: In response to hearing about a friend's child's or grandchild's trip to Washington with a school class, the hostile person interrupts, "Let me tell you about my niece's trip to France two years ago."

This focus on self, including information gathering, judgments, advice, and lack of real and concentrated attention to what others are actually saying, is one of the main reasons for the angry interchanges so frequent in a hostile person's life. It probably accounts for the nonverbal body language during interviews that

John Barefoot found provided the best clues to the hostility level of the person being interviewed.

To reduce the escalation of angry responses, as well as to encourage more positive interchanges, you must learn simply to listen.

How to Use This Strategy

All you have to do at first is listen. As we said, it's that simple. While the other person is talking, look him or her straight in the eyes, lean toward him or her with an intent expression of interest as well as a positive facial expression, and *never* interrupt—*always* wait until the other person is finished speaking before you say a word.

At first, of course, your mind will not be very firmly oriented toward the other person's words. You will be preoccupied as usual with your own thoughts and associations to whatever the person has said. Don't be surprised when this happens—it's normal. The important thing is to fight the urge to break in with your own brilliant comments. Instead, shift your attention away from your own thoughts, back to whatever the other person is saying.

You may be thinking that this sounds a lot like what you learned as the meditation strategy. That's right. Think of listening as a form of meditation. Instead of paying attention to your own breathing and repeating a word every time you breathe out, in listening you attend to the other person and his or her words. And when your attention wanders to your own thoughts, *just as in meditation,* don't let that bother you; simply bring your attention back to the primary matter at hand—the other person.

Do this, and the rest will follow.

That is, you will develop the ability to understand not only the surface content but also the underlying message he or she is trying to get across. Thus, when someone is gushing about all the scholarly accomplishments of his or her grandchild, instead of breaking in to top that with your own grandchild, the time will come when you will know to wait until the person has finished the story about the grandchild and then say, "That's wonderful! I know you must be very proud."

To be a good listener, you will have to steer clear of some pitfalls. Avoid being *judgmental.* Constantly monitor your consciousness. Every time you begin to judge the speaker, silently yell "Stop!" and immediately refocus your attention on what the speaker is saying.

The objective information the speaker is telling you also carries an important emotional message. You do not need to determine all the facts right away. Resist the temptation to turn the conversation into an immediate *grill*.

After listening for a short while, you may think that you have excellent information or *advice*. Resist all urges to share your wisdom! You may not yet have the necessary facts. You may not yet appreciate the emotional content of what that person is telling you. Even if you are correct, your well-intentioned advice may not be appreciated; the speaker may want your empathy, not your solutions. You can at a later time give the speaker advice if you still deem it appropriate. For now, keep your advice to yourself.

As a final part of listening, after the speaker has finished, try to reflect back what you heard. The simplest way to do this is to repeat in your own words what you understood was said. "Do you mean that . . . ?"

On a few occasions, you may want to ask some clarification questions and eventually summarize.

After your initial response, return to the listening mode while the other person lets you know if your version corresponds to his or hers. If it does not, your remarks have let the other person know that he or she needs to try again to explain more clearly. This way, once you have indeed understood, the other person will know it and be able now to let you respond.

Being a good listener does not mean that you can't *in turn* be an equally good speaker. Indeed, you may find the other person receptive to listening to what you have to say, now that you've listened. Do remember to stick to the issue already under discussion.

Don't be surprised if listening improves your relationships. When you reflect what you have heard, you have yourself communicated a very powerful message: "I can really hear what you are saying."

Why This Strategy Works

Larry Scherwitz, a psychologist, has found that persons who are more self-involved have more severe coronary disease than their less self-involved counterparts. He studied 150 patients hospitalized for suspected heart disease or after a heart attack by monitoring how often they used *I, me, my, mine,* or *myself* during a structured interview designed to evaluate whether they were Type A. He found that patients with more severe disease gave longer answers and hence had more self references.

Scherwitz's findings remained significant even when he matched patients for age, blood pressure, cholesterol, and Type A behavior. Scherwitz was also able to discount the illness itself as explanation, as his correlations were stronger in patients with no previous heart attack and no angina.

A hostile person's distrust for others probably leads him or her to focus almost exclusively on his or her own thoughts and ideas. In learning to be a good listener, you can break out of this locked-in focus on yourself.

Listening is a foolproof strategy almost *guaranteed* to succeed. At first, you just force yourself to keep your mouth shut, lean forward, and look intently at the other person. With time this simple "meditationlike" behavioral change—attending to the other person and every time your mind wanders bringing it back to his or her words—will enable you to expand your ability to not only hear the words but also to *understand* the message those words convey.

Listening decreases the likelihood of arguments. Equally important, it serves a general purpose of increasing the likelihood that others will experience their interactions with you as positive. Thus, listening becomes self-reinforcing; it makes others seek your company.

Besides these benefits related to reducing your hostility, there are other, more far-reaching dividends for the hostile person who becomes a good listener. Because you already know everything you already know, you will, by being able to hear, and thereby absorb, what other people know, learn *new things.*

These benefits are not, of course, the result of some new discovery of ours. More than two thousand years ago, Jewish sages were telling us, "Silence is good for the wise; how much more so for the foolish. . . . Even a fool, when he holdeth his peace, is counted wise" (Proverbs 17:28). And Confucius told us, "A gentleman (i.e., a good man) covets the reputation of being slow in word but prompt in deed" (Analects IV: 24). By keeping our silence when others are speaking, we not only give the appearance of valuing their words but also, by following this practice, open ourselves to adding to our wisdom.

———

Both of us have always liked working and telling each other about what we are doing. A problem arose in the early 1980s. Redford was excited by his research showing the importance of hostility, and Virginia took a new job. As always, when we first got home each day, we would sit down to talk for a few minutes. Virginia felt that during these exchanges she never got a word in edgewise. She felt that Redford kept interrupting, not listening. She also felt that he kept switching the topic back to his work when she wanted a chance to talk about *her* work.

Virginia's growing resentment over this made her increasingly often tune out what Redford was saying, and this made him resent her lack of interest in what interested him. For several months, we each felt unappreciated. Once we shared our feelings about this, we realized a solution that, although artificial and temporary, worked for us. Virginia would have the first five minutes or so, with Redford attentively listening during that time. Then Redford would get his turn, and Virginia would listen.

In our workshops, we always include listening exercises. For example, each member of a pair has five minutes to talk without interruption about anything on his or her mind. The other person listens intently and then reflects what he or she heard. Our workshop participants are amazed at how much fun this exercise is—to actually have someone's undivided attention.

Participants *usually* remark spontaneously that their partner is interesting, likable, or humorous. They achieve this new perspective whether they are the listener who afterward reflects what was heard, speaker, or both. This simple assignment has on at least one occasion led to matchmaking.

When we asked participants in one workshop to practice the Listen strategy with a stranger as a homework assignment, several came back next session with reports that they had been able to make a new friend, experienced the other as more accepting of them, and the like.

THE ABCS OF LISTENING

A. Decide that in conversation with others you are going to decrease your habit of focusing mainly on your own associations and thoughts that are stimulated by the other's words. Instead, you are going to concentrate on developing your listening skills.

B. When talking with someone else, force yourself to keep your silence while you focus all your attention, both mental and physical, on the other person. Before speaking your own mind, first repeat to the other person what you understand his or her message to be. Then give the other person a chance to let you know if your understanding is correct.

C. As you begin to use this strategy, notice how it changes the quality of your interactions. Congratulate yourself on this simple but real accomplishment. As time passes and your ability to understand the messages embedded in other people's words grows, enjoy the new world opened up to you.

EXERCISES

1. Pick likely encounters in the future when you will plan to go into your "listening mode" with the following types of people:

    A. a stranger

    B. a friend or co-worker

    C. a child or parent

    D. a spouse or other good friend

After each of these actual encounters, try to identify how using the technique of listening differs from similar encounters when you are in your normal "me first" mode.

2. Arrange with your partner for one of you to speak for ten minutes. Use a timer if you have to. The other person only listens with undivided attention, saying nothing. Switch roles and repeat. In this exercise, you need not reflect what you have heard, but only listen.

3. After listening to a friend or acquaintance you will see again soon, make some notes on what was said of ongoing importance. Before the next time you see this person, review your notes so that you can express your continued interest in the matter. In fact, you probably will be more interested because of the extra attention you have devoted to the topic. Certainly, your friend or acquaintance will feel listened to and valued.

"Because my genetic programming prevents me from
stopping to ask directions—that's why!"

CHAPTER 11

Practice Trusting Others

"Our goal is progress, not perfection."
Redford and Virginia Williams, twentieth-century realists

CALVIN AND HOBBES copyright 1991. Distributed by Universal Press Syndicate.
Reprinted with permission. All rights reserved.

GENERAL PRINCIPLES

When to Use This Strategy

One of the major obstacles we hostile people face in reducing our hostility is our basic mistrust of other people. Because we think that others are selfish, mean, and brutish, we usually depend on ourselves in any situation we encounter in daily life, even in the most trivial matters. We *fear* the consequences if we trust even the person at the seafood counter to pick out a tuna steak for us. This fear can assume terrifying proportions as we deal with personal, community, and even international affairs—almost as though there were a trap door beneath our feet that would suddenly fly open to plunge us into a pit of ravenous alligators if we mistakenly trusted someone!

If you learn to trust others, you can forgo the constant, often exhausting alertness for their misbehavior. You will find yourself in fewer situations in which you perceive others as acting badly, and this in turn will reduce your number of angry outbursts. Conquering your basic mistrust of others is an extremely effective but very difficult-to-achieve means of controlling your hostility. You will probably never succeed completely. With the techniques in this chapter, though, you can make significant progress in overcoming your fears.

How to Use This Strategy

Force yourself to relinquish control. Begin by identifying some situations you consider inconsequential. Instead of taking charge as you usually do, simply ask (or let) another person to take control (pick out the tuna steak, choose the seat on the plane, toss the salad, drive the car, or whatever).

On some occasions you'll end up with a better choice or better state of affairs. Most often, nothing disastrous will happen. Experience how truly liberating it can be for you to have lifted from your shoulders the awesome burden of having to be in charge of every situation every single minute of your life!

Don't count on these experiences to come easily. You likely will remain hypercritical of others and extremely anxious whenever you relinquish control. The anxiety should diminish with increasing exposure.

As a next step, extend yourself to trusting the other person in ever more scary situations. Let your partner choose your birthday present. Let someone besides yourself select the restaurant. If you usually prepare meals, trust the other person to fix dinner. You will know you are making real progress when you can let your spouse actually drive the car or boat without your help as self-appointed co-pilot.

Another special application merits your consideration. Participants in our workshops report delightful results when they have been able to extend trusting others into their bedrooms. If you're usually the more active partner in lovemaking, consider asking your lover to assume control of all aspects of the next encounter, including initiation, caressing, and any fantasy play. If intercourse is part of your usual lovemaking, on this special occasion, let your partner also decide if this encounter will result in intercourse; if so, let the timing be under your partner's control.

When under stress, you will probably backslide. This is normal.

Believe us, this experience of trusting another person and finding that it's *okay* can be one of the most liberating steps a hostile person ever takes. Trusting your spouse at first in little matters and eventually with your innermost thoughts can help to reinforce the intimacy most of us would like to experience in our marriage. Practicing trust should improve your other relationships as well.

Why This Strategy Works

Basically, hostile people can even be considered *phobic* when it comes to trusting others. One long-established treatment for overcoming phobias is the behavior modification technique of systematic desensitization. By exposing yourself to a feared situation, beginning with relatively trivial examples and progressing to more important circumstances, you will see for yourself that the feared consequences (the trap door and the alligator pit) do not occur. You can gradually learn that you don't need to be so fearful of the situation.

Jim Henry of Loma Linda University is one of the premier investigators of the relationship between the brain and behavior. Virginia corresponds with him on occasion about topics of mutual interest. In a recent letter to Jim, she suggested that maybe biology can now allow for free will. If our brain is composed of our entire evolutionary heritage, for any stimulus we are likely to have many possible responses. If we will pause to consider all of our reactions, we are then free to choose among them.

Jim took Virginia's musings one step further to speculate that some of our patterns of behavior like rage, fear, and despair depend on the old reptilian brain, that is, the brainstem and the limbic system. These are the bases of self-preservative behaviors.

Then there are the more recently evolved mammalian species-preservative behaviors: attachment, mother-infant bonding, speech, and play. The extent of one's hostility might be an expression of the degree to which one feels threatened and insecure. Jim says this appears to be a state in which there is alexithymic feeling loss and the species-preservative patterns of the right hemisphere are suppressed. Within the framework of Jim and Virginia's speculations, successful efforts to trust others when the first inclination is otherwise becomes a willful decision not to feel threatened and insecure and hence at the mercy of the reptilian part of the brain.

Some of the benefits of trusting others require no speculations. Most of the time, the consequences of relinquishing control are not as bad as you had feared—your tuna steak will be just fine; you'll arrive at your destination safely; and so on. By experiencing this lack of dire consequences, you will find that your fear of trusting others will gradually lessen. Over time, you will begin to find it easier to trust, even when it comes to bigger things in life.

By learning to trust others, you can increase the inner strength that comes from strong social support. Ross Perot's 1992 running mate and Navy Commander James Bond Stockdale was a prisoner of war in Vietnam for seven years. Now a senior research fellow at the Hoover Institution at Stanford, he maintains that POWs should learn to rely on other captives to survive imprisonment. "The number-one personality trait that spelled disaster and heartbreak and failure was not trusting in your [fellow captives]. . . . The highest value in prison isn't God or country, it's the guy next door. You've got to stick together. It's all you've got."

Think about distrust among nations. How many of our international tensions and actual conflicts are a result of each country's needing to be in control? How often does each country perceive other nations as full of evil intentions?

THE ABCS OF TRUSTING OTHERS

A. Identify some relatively inconsequential situation in which you usually try to take control.

B. The next time you are in that situation, instead of taking charge as is your wont, simply tell the other person to go ahead and make the choice.

C. Notice that nothing terrible happens when you let the other person take charge. Repeat trusting on every possible similar occasion. Extend trusting to scarier situations.

EXERCISES

1. Make a list of matters you prefer to attend to yourself. Look at the list carefully and see if any of the activities could be occasionally taken over by your spouse, a friend, a co-worker, and/or your children.

2. As an extension, think internationally. Ponder how much of your attitudes toward other nations may be primarily based on your own cynical mistrust rather than their behavior.

CHAPTER 12

Take on
Community Service

"If I am not in my own behalf, who will be in my behalf?
And if I am for myself only, what am I?
And if not in the present, when?"
                    Hillel,
                    first-century B.C. to A.D. Jewish sage

GENERAL PRINCIPLES

When to Use This Strategy

Donating your time for public service is another strategy for reducing your isolation and alienation. When you take on community service, you reinforce your sense of connectedness with other people.

Taking on community service will improve your skills in caring for others by providing you with real-life experiences in altruistic behaviors. By taking on a community service in which you volunteer to help other individuals or groups, you will not only be learning specific caring behaviors but also enlarging your capacity for heartfelt empathy and reducing your social isolation.

How to Use This Strategy

In *The Healing Power of Doing Good,* Allan Luks, a professional volunteer coordinator, offers would-be volunteers practical suggestions that he says will increase the effectiveness of proffered help, as well as the health and spiritual benefits to the helpers:

- Look for situations that include personal contact with the individuals who need the help.

- Seek out opportunities that involve about two hours a week of one-to-one helping.

- Try to help strangers. You are less likely to overextend yourself; also, these kinds of contacts break down feelings of "us" and "them."

- Look for problem areas where you can easily empathize with the people you hope to help.

- Look for a supportive formal organization, which facilitates access to strangers, a regular schedule, and a sense of teamwork.

- Find a service that uses a skill you have or that gives you the training you'll need.

- Exert yourself to reach out. Your efforts should require a significant extension of yourself, either physically or emotionally.

- Forget the benefits you expect to give or receive. You must simply enjoy the feeling of closeness to the person you're trying to help.

Obviously, working with the homeless exposes you to more heartrending stories than helping in a school library. Signing on for an evening a week for six months locks you in more than showing up whenever you wish. First consider Luks's guidelines. Then consider your own preferences before you decide on the initial level of commitment you want. When you are ready, seek those activities in your community that interest you most and also fit your level of commitment. Be as realistic as you can; stretch a bit, but you will gain little by volunteering more time than you can realistically spare or by exposing yourself to a group you are deeply turned off by or deeply afraid of.

At the end of this chapter is a preliminary Exercise to help you begin to think about possible options. Go with what interests you.

As the next step after reading our list, identify the service opportunities in your areas of interest available in your locality. Across the nation, several different organizations are involved in matching up volunteers with helping associations. In many communities, all you need to do is contact your Volunteer Center, which coordinates all community services. In most communities, your local United Way can function as a referral center. A few county and city libraries have notebooks listing the names, addresses, and phone numbers of all community services. If none of these possibilities for connecting up with a local group in your area of interest is available in your community, contact Points of Light, a national organization located in Washington, D.C. (telephone [800] 879-5400).

Once you know what your local options are, pick one or more and call them up to get direct information about their services. You may next want to visit their place of operations to observe their activities. Don't hesitate to ask questions. Once you are ready, volunteer. Feel free to limit your offer of services. You'll probably be warmly welcomed. If not, move on to volunteer with your second choice.

As you participate in the helping mission of the group you have chosen, try to practice some of the other strategies—listening, practicing empathy, and practicing tolerance, for example.

Enjoy any positive feedback. Also draw on the social support that will be available to you as you become part of a group of committed people who are trying to ease the plight of those with difficulties in their lives. Celebrate your accomplishment in being able both to see beyond your own personal needs and wants to those of others *and* to do something concrete about it.

Why This Strategy Works

Most of us assume the identity society gives us or feel shackled to the image our behavior creates. By choice, however, we can give ourselves a helping, warm-hearted identity simply by placing ourselves in structured helping situations. An experiment conducted a number of years ago illustrates the power an imposed identity can have. To study the effect of prisons, a number of experimental subjects were actually placed in a prison environment. Some subjects were assigned the role of guards, and others became the prisoners. Within a short span of time in this prison setting, the new "guards" had become brutal, and the behavior of the new "prisoners" had regressed to a more dependent, childlike pattern. These behavioral changes all occurred in people who did not have these particular characteristics before the experiment began! In contrast with the prison experiment, when you assume the role of helper, you are likely to *grow* to fit the assigned role.

Altruism may help you live longer. Extending yourself to interact with others is associated with longevity. Twenty-seven hundred people in Tecumseh, Michigan, were given a round of interviews about their social relationships as well as medical exams by James House, a sociologist, and his colleagues at the University of Michigan Survey Research Center. These subjects were followed for the next ten years. Men who attended fewer than one voluntary meeting a week died at a significantly greater rate than more active men, even when the effects of age and a variety of risk factors for mortality were taken into account. This association between longevity and voluntary meetings is less clear for women.

Another study examined more than three thousand volunteers who completed questionnaires about their volunteer activities and state of health. Howard Andrews of New York State Psychiatric Institute and the Department of Neurology at Columbia found volunteering associated with self-reports of better health even after adjusting for age, sex, and marital status. Benefits were greatest for volunteers who helped strangers and who volunteered frequently.

Two psychologists, Karen Kendall and Mary Beth Kenkel, wanted to find out what people who volunteered a great deal of their time and/or money got out of it. They studied nineteen such individuals in a rural Oklahoma community by face-to-face interviews, questionnaires, and an exit telephone interview. Sixteen of these nineteen heavily involved volunteers were physically tired and emotionally drained by their efforts. Fourteen were in need of spiritual guidance themselves as a result, the same number who had often reached the point that they cut back or quit for a while.

Given these significant costs, what did these volunteers get? Seventeen respondents said that helping was important to their self-image. An equal number said that aid had been provided them by people previously assisted. Nine respondents were pleased with their accomplishments, and getting their own social needs met was mentioned equally often. All who were interviewed said that they found volunteering more enjoyable and satisfying when appreciation was expressed.

The so-called "helper's high" of volunteering cannot yet be explained, although a number of logical theories have been put forth. One we consider a good bet is that volunteering increases your sources of social support.

Helping those who are less fortunate should be especially health promoting, as doing so is an excellent means of controlling one's cynicism and the resulting angry thoughts and actions. Basic mistrust often leads us hostile people to view entire groups with suspicion and disdain: "The homeless are just too lazy to get a job," for example, or "Most old folks ought to be put away." Getting to know on a more intimate level those who are members of whole categories of people we formerly dismissed can help us to see them as the real human beings they actually are—people with hopes, concerns, needs, wants, shortcomings, and fears that are often similar to our own.

The community soup kitchen in Durham, North Carolina, provides three meals a day to about two hundred people. Food preparation, serving, and cleanup are handled by a combination of paid employees, volunteers, and minor offenders assigned hours of community service by the courts.

We talked to members of the first two groups of helpers, who usually experience the satisfaction and enjoyment they expected to find.

"It's a pretty good job." [When pressed, he adds,] "I like feeding people who need it."

"I get to use my sales experience. And I don't take the job home with me. I cut it off at the door. I enjoy doing a good job."

"It's part of my [religious] witness."

"I've gotten a lot from many different people at various times in my life. This is my way of giving something back."

"We tell our sons to be involved, so I need to practice what I preach."

"It broadens my exposure. I meet different kinds of people here. That's interesting."

"I like the people I meet."

Sometimes, even the offenders doing community service gain more than freedom from incarceration.

"Sitting at home watching TV all the time gets boring. I feel better when I get out and do something."

"I guess I don't have it as bad as some people."

"The work ain't much because it's the same thing every day. But the people here are fine."

"It's not so bad. It's not as hard [work] as I thought it would be. And the people: They're friendly and all."

THE ABCS OF TAKING ON COMMUNITY SERVICE

A. Decide that you need to reduce your isolation by taking on community service.

B. Choose a community group and volunteer your time.

C. Use your experiences as a volunteer to practice some of the hostility-reducing strategies you have learned already in this book. Also, take advantage of contacts with co-volunteers and those you are helping as an opportunity to increase your empathic skills.

EXERCISES

Review the following list of community-service groups and put a check by every activity that appeals, even a little bit.

Abuse of Spouse or Child
Child Advocacy Commission, Child and Parent Support Services, Coalition for Battered Women, Rape Crisis Center, Women's Center

Adoption
Children's homes, expectant mothers' homes, international social services, groups on adolescent pregnancy

Alcohol and Drug Abuse
Lobbying groups advocating governmental actions, public-information groups, residential programs

Blood Services
American Red Cross

Causes
Habitat for Humanity, Sierra Club, and so on.

Child Care
Day and after-school care
Adolescent education scholarship funds, child-care networks, child-care resource and referral groups, day-care services associations, court child-care and family services programs, Head Start programs, YMCA programs

Developmental/special needs of children
Association for retarded citizens, learning centers, residential centers

Conservation
50 Things You Can Do To Save the Earth (The Earth Works Group, Berkeley, CA 94709), 94–5 lists a number of groups from around the country that are actively involved.

Crisis Intervention/Treatment
Community guidance clinics, crisis hotlines, dispute-settlement centers, family counseling services, residential programs, teen medical services

Developmentally Disabled
Autism Society, Epilepsy Association, Goodwill Industries, rehabilitation programs, residential programs, retarded programs under child care, schools for people with special needs

Disaster Relief
American Red Cross, Congregations in Mission, Salvation Army

Elderly Services
Councils on Aging, Meals on Wheels, Salvation Army, YMCA, YWCA

Food/Nutrition
Child-care networks, child-care resource and referral centers, day-care services associations, food banks, homeless shelters, Interfaith Council, Meals on Wheels for shut-ins, soup kitchens

Government
League of Women Voters, local offices of elected officials, political campaigns

Hearing Impaired
Developmental programs, diagnostic centers

Home Health Care
Direct medical funds, hospice, senior-citizen programs

Housing Needs
Assistance in obtaining housing, maintenance/repair, rent/fuel/utilities, temporary shelter

Individual/Family Counseling
Associations for groups with special needs, community guidance clinics, family counseling, financial counseling, hospice, Interfaith Council, Mental Health Association, youth counseling

Job Counseling/Training/Placement
Disabled groups, disadvantaged groups, general programs

Legal Services
Child advocacy, general programs, senior citizen programs, women's center

Medical Services/Medical Rehabilitation
Direct medical funds; hospital volunteer programs like children's ward, nursery, or cancer support programs

Mental-Health Services
Alcohol/drug councils, counseling services, life enrichment centers, residential programs

Physical Health/Safety/Education
See alcohol/drug abuse listing, American Red Cross, YMCA

Recycling/Environmental Groups
Earthworm, 186 South Street, Boston MA 02111, telephone (617) 426-7344 has a hotline for finding and establishing recycling programs.

Religious Groups
Churches, synagogues, mosques, temples; see also chapter 18.

Respite Care
Hospice, retarded programs, aged programs, including senior daycare centers

Rest Homes
Many residents have few visitors.

Schools
Classrooms, libraries, parent groups

Service Clubs
Jaycees, Lions, Rotary

Teen Services
Boy Scouts, Girl Scouts, Teen Hopeline, runaway programs

Transportation
American Red Cross for dialysis, senior-citizen programs

Traveler's Aid

Tutoring
Illiterate adults, schoolchildren

Volunteer Firefighters and Ambulance Helpers
Available in rural communities

Visually Impaired

Women's Services
Battered women services, rape crisis centers, women's centers

Youth Programs/Recreation/Camps
Boy Scouts, Boys Club, community centers, 4-H programs, Girl Scouts, Girls Club, Salvation Army Boys and Girls Club, YMCA, YWCA

You will see that the list contains some opportunities to help people rather like yourself but also includes people in your community with whom you probably have little contact. The wider the circle of people you have direct contact with, the more opportunities there will be for you to see perspectives and people with backgrounds and circumstances quite different from your own. Because some of these people will undoubtedly be from groups your hostility has led you to dismiss or dislike in the past, you may be able to change this negative view—to become more empathetic—by increasing your personal contact with them.

Therefore, we suggest that as you explore local options, you volunteer to work in your community with an organization that not only interests you and is within your comfort level but that also brings you into contact with a group that is most different from the people you see ordinarily.

CHAPTER 13

Increase Your Empathy

"To each foot, its own shoe."
Montaigne, sixteenth-century French philosopher

CALVIN AND HOBBES copyright 1986. Distributed by Universal Press Syndicate.
Reprinted with permission. All rights reserved.

GENERAL PRINCIPLES

When to Use This Strategy

The strategies you have been learning about in the last few chapters will increase your sensitivity toward other people. From this base you can proceed to develop empathy—the ability to project oneself into the consciousness of another person, to thus better understand the motivations of others and reduce the intrusiveness of mistrust when it comes to making judgments about their behavior. Now, rather than coming at the issue of empathy indirectly, in this chapter we will provide more direct ways to increase your sympathetic understanding of others.

Try the empathy strategy whenever you find yourself reaching a negative evaluation of the motives of another person—whether a stranger you don't even see, a stranger you do see, or a close friend or relative. Perhaps your child's teacher is overwhelmed by his first job and not at all a vicious person? Could the parent with the grocery cart full of junk food have been raised that way herself or be ignorant about nutrition? Instead of reacting negatively to your spouse's ill humor, can you find out what's bothering him or her?

How to Use This Strategy

The application of empathy involves an extension of the reason-with-yourself approach already described in chapter 3. There, you learned how to carry on an internal dialogue as a means of talking yourself out of petty or unjustified hostile thoughts, feelings, or urges, as well as even justified hostility when you have no effective response available.

You can use this same sort of internal dialogue to step into the other person's shoes, to experience the situation from his or her perspective.

Instead of assuming that another's motives are evil, to be more empathic play out in your head various scenarios in which his or her behavior would be acceptable. For example, if you are waiting in a bank line because the woman in front of you is slow, consider legitimate reasons why she is taking so long. Maybe she is ill, senile, or simply not as quick as she once was. Do these considerations make you less annoyed at her?

As another example, focus on other drivers. Sometimes they may not see or hear as well as you. Their reaction times may not be as quick. Try to imagine driving under the more restrictive conditions they must face. When you make their skills your focus, your ire at their "inconsideration" may diminish.

Focusing yet more widely, think about other nations. Like the United States, other countries may have their own fears, priorities, and national goals. Try to imagine their own internal political groups often competing among themselves for power. Foreigners, like us, also have a mixture of public and private motivations. Try to imagine them as family people. Try to think about what their personal priorities likely are.

Every time you can see another person or group from their own perspective, your ability to empathize will grow. And as your empathic skill increases, you will have gained another weapon in your anti-hostility arsenal.

This technique can almost always work for talking yourself out of hostile thoughts, feelings, or urges toward individuals you have little contact with. Because your own inference that they are behaving out of evil motives cannot be proven, you should be able to convince yourself that they could just as easily have an acceptable reason for their behavior.

With practice over time, improved empathic skills can help you sort out those situations in which your cynical beliefs about motives should be discarded. When you are able to do this, the harm you do in relationships with those you care about will decrease.

Eventually, you may decide that foreigners have interests and goals beyond being our national enemies.

Sometimes, of course, you will be unable to find a reasonable motive for the behavior of the other person or nation. It's possible that there is *not* a reasonable motive and that the behavior *is* hostile. In this case, empathy leads you to conclude that it was not your but the other person's hostility that is responsible for your ire. Having reached this conclusion, you will need, of course, to move on to another strategy. Depending upon the specific circumstances, assertion may be called for.

Why This Strategy Works

By being able to see a situation through another person's eyes, you will often find yourself able to short circuit cynical beliefs before they generate the anger that is harmful to your health or causes you to act out the impulses that harm your relationships. Because your conclusion that another person is behaving badly is more often the result of your own beliefs than it is of his or her actual motives and actions, you can count on some success in talking yourself out of your anger by convincing yourself that the other person's behavior is just as likely to be reasonable as it is to be selfish.

Just as important, by not lashing out at another person based on your often erroneous beliefs and by instead allowing your empathy to cause you to respond in a more helping manner, you will find that others will begin to treat you better as well.

Reacting with empathy instead of with negativity will reinforce your own positive healthful behaviors. A series of experiments from the 1960s corroborates this. Third graders were frustrated by some sixth-grade "helpers" as they tried to complete an assigned task. Afterward they were given randomly assigned opportunities for aggressive play, social talk, or a reasonable explanation by the experimenter of why the sixth graders had behaved as they had.

Frustration always led to heightened aggressive feelings among these eight- and nine-year-old subjects, but what group they had been assigned to determined how aggressive they felt. Those in the group assigned to aggressive play were told that when they pushed a button, they would be administering a small electric shock to their sixth-grade "helpers." (Of course, no shock was really administered.)

The aggressive feelings among the third graders who thought they had administered an actual shock were not reduced! Likewise, the "social talk" group that rated how much they liked or disliked the frustrators actually *increased* their aggressive feelings. Only the third group of students had their aggressive feelings strikingly reduced, when they listened to a reasonable interpretation of their frustrators' behavior, which explanation of course helped them to empathize.

In another experiment in the 1970s, male college students had their blood pressure measured when performing a task. They were always harassed by a rude, obnoxious experimenter while they were trying to complete the assigned task. Some subjects were told that the experimenter was uptight about an important exam; others were told nothing. Some of the group were informed about the extenuating circumstances beforehand, others after the experimenter was rude. Blood-pressure changes were greatest when subjects were given no information, least when they were given the prior information that helped to explain the experimenter's misbehavior when it occurred. This experiment shows directly that increasing empathy lessens the biologic cost.

The first autumn after we were married, Redford began medical school and Virginia started her first teaching job. Time was tight, and the dirty linens and clothes would pile up until one of us—usually Virginia—took them to the public laundromat.

This particular evening, after teaching all day, Virginia had gone to the laundromat to wash and dry numerous loads. She finished after dark, then went home to start preparing supper, dropping the laundry basket on the kitchen floor as she came in.

Redford worked late at the medical school, and by the time he reached home, the spaghetti sauce was almost ready. He walked in, briefly greeted Virginia, and immediately walked over to the basket of folded laundry to feel the towels on top. Still damp!

Redford saw red. "These towels are still damp!" he pointed out. After more grousing about doing the job right, he picked up the basket and stormed back to the laundromat, where *he* would get the clothes dried properly. Virginia said nothing but shot him a malicious look as he departed.

By the time he returned, Virginia was hurt, angry, and resolved to let the laundry mold from now on. Redford was in a foul mood also, angry at Virginia for what he saw as her incompetence, hungry, and tired. The evening was ruined.

With less cynical mistrust of others, Redford might never have felt the laundry. With more assertive skills, Virginia might have better communicated her perspective.

Redford also could have practiced empathy. Virginia had taught all day, then stopped to do the laundry. He could have defused his anger by telling himself that she was probably already exhausted even before she got to the laundromat.

His perspective would have shifted from Virginia's "incompetence" to sympathy with how tired she was: "You poor dear. You must be really wiped out from both teaching all day and then doing the laundry."

Virginia could then have rejoindered that she was about to drop and had been too wiped out for another drying cycle. We could have hung the almost-dry towels in the bathroom and enjoyed the spaghetti dinner. We could have discussed, when we were rested, how we were going to keep on top of the laundry with so little free time.

But this was our first year of living together, and we both still had a lot to learn about empathy, trust, and assertion.

THE ABCS OF INCREASING YOUR
EMPATHY

A. Realizing that many times your evaluation of the motives of others may not be valid, decide to try to increase your empathic skills.

B. Whenever you find yourself with hostile thoughts, feelings, or urges stimulated by another's behavior, begin an internal dialogue in which you try to convince yourself that the other person's behavior may be reasonable and justified rather than selfishly motivated.

C. Every time you are able to defuse this hostility by changing your judgment of others' motives, celebrate your success in your increasing mastery.

EXERCISES

1. In each of the following situations, conduct a dialogue with yourself to see if you can think of three reasonable motivations for the behavior described.

    A. The man ahead of you in the checkout line is paying for his entire purchase with coins.

    B. Your friend fails to show up at the agreed-upon time to give you a needed ride. When she does finally arrive, she explains that an important phone call came through just before it was time to pick you up.

2. Select the senatorial or presidential candidate you voted *against* in the last election. Can you articulate effectively the case *for* supporting that person?

CHAPTER **14**

Be Tolerant

"To have doubted one's own first principles is the mark of a civilized man."

Oliver Wendell Holmes Jr.,
nineteenth- and twentieth-century U.S. jurist

GENERAL PRINCIPLES

When to Use This Strategy

The tolerance strategy is for people who are too frequently right, which is most of us at least some of the time. We may be able to listen for a while. We may even be able to empathize temporarily. But in the end we can't take the additional permanent step of allowing other people to have beliefs, practices, and habits different from our own.

When we are intolerant, we perceive others as misbehaving. And most of the time when this happens, we become angry.

Sometimes tolerance is inappropriate. By all means, protect yourself and what you hold dear whenever you need to. Anger that is genuinely justifiable acts as a powerful tool for personal and social justice. Practice assertion and contribute money and/or time to counter the evil you see around you.

On the other hand, tolerance (or, with our intimates, nonjudgmental acceptance) is frequently the preferable course of action. People who are frequently judgmental feel virtuous, but their bodies (and souls) pay a very heavy price. Whenever they disapprove of the misbehavior of another, they become isolated from that person. The more frequent their disapproval, the more extensive their estrangement. The resultant social isolation, as we learned earlier, places their health at risk.

Perhaps your judgments are directed toward people close to

"Just hear me out, then tell me I'm wrong."

you, who must conform to your standards or experience your disapproval or even wrath. Do you decide what the behaviors of the people important to you should be and then become angry with them when they don't measure up?

We all are often tempted to insist that our intimates behave as we wish. Perhaps you are angry because of your own conclusions that your spouse could better control his or her intake of cholesterol and fat, is wrong to give priority to the bowling match over the Little League game, or is behaving unacceptably when he or she refuses to go to religious services. A judgmental person also wants to be the one to decide how clean the house will be, how ambitious the spouse ought to be, and how much the other person should relax.

Maybe your righteousness is directed toward your offspring. You are angry because your child doesn't make the honor roll, get all A's, limit use of makeup, throw away the rock 'n' roll wardrobe, or spruce up. Or perhaps your attitude is directed toward people at work. If none of these examples of judgments of the behavior of your intimate acquaintances fits your situation, try to come up with your own list.

For others of us, our intolerance is directed toward casual acquaintances or even people we have never met. Are many of the people you see or read about each day naïve, stupid, lazy, morally underdeveloped, unenlightened, or pigheaded? They should act differently, as they ought to be able to see the folly of their ways, but they don't. They behave badly in public. They continue to hold the same asinine political opinions. They remain wrong in their religious beliefs. They cause wars your country then has to fight. Again, expand this list with your own examples as needed.

Use the tolerance strategy to reexamine all the entries in your Hostility Log that you labeled justifiable anger. Maybe you can transfer a few over into the unjustified column and resolve the next time you are in a similar situation to practice tolerance by accepting the other person (or group) as he or she presently is. Remember, every time you do this, you will effectively eliminate your anger!

How to Use This Strategy

All you have to do to practice tolerance is to *accept other people as they are, not as you would like them to be.*

You already know how to gather the objective facts in a situation generating your hostility (chapter 3, "Reason with Yourself").

You already have learned in all your interactions to listen (chapter 10, "Listen!").

You also are trying to learn to see the other person's perspective (chapter 13, "Increase Your Empathy").

Now take some additional steps by applying all these other skills with two additional questions:

1. Is the other person consciously malevolent or *from his or her perspective* acting in good faith?

2. Is the position different from your own reached by the other person reasonable, *from his or her perspective*?

Note that you are not asking if this perspective is *justified,* but only if the other perspective is *reasonable.* An example may help here. Recall Redford's experience with his recently arrived New York colleague as described in chapter 8. Redford chose in that situation to use the assertion strategy as a means of getting his colleague to use less abrasive language. He could also have tried to practice *tolerance.*

"Of course," Redford might have mused to himself, "Sam is certainly not *justified* in labeling my idea 'ridiculous,' but I suppose it may be a *reasonable* word choice, if I view it from *his* perspective. After all, in New York City you expect to hear vivid speech, not our more restrained southern style. He doesn't intend to be mean to me—that's just the way he learned to carry on a conversation."

As the next and most crucial step, *try to allow the other person to be different.* In other words, *accept other people as they are.* Redford, continuing his application of this strategy, might conclude, "Hey, that's just the way New Yorkers talk normally. Sam is no more intending to be nasty to me than an effusive southerner would be intending to make a pass at a strange woman if he smiled a cheery 'Good morning!' at her as he held the door open. I really do know that Sam's one of my best friends. I just need to realize that it's his normal mode of expression to say 'That's ridiculous!' instead of an intended insult."

Sometimes true justice won't be sacrificed by tolerance. Self-justified anger is often generated not on behalf of what is right but by our inability initially to consider both our own fallibility and the possibility of perspectives other than our own.

Sometimes when you know you are in the right, other objective observers may not be so certain. King Solomon in all his wisdom might have to ponder for a long while whatever is at issue and then still might not be confident in deciding what was right, given the differences of perspectives and the complexity of the many issues involved.

Even when you are absolutely right, King Solomon might prefer that you keep anger at bay. The other party may still deserve to be treated generously, as he or she may honestly be misguided, not malevolent or bent on destruction. Tolerance may indeed be wise, either because the situation is inconsequential or because tolerance will lead to the best eventual outcome for everyone.

Why This Strategy Works

Every time you succeed in allowing another to be different from you, you will dissipate your anger!

Even if in the end you can't accept the other person as he or she is, just the process of trying to practice tolerance can benefit you.

- As long as you are continuing to consider the situation from the other party's perspective, you have not yet concluded the situation is an important threat necessitating a fight-or-flight response. If you succeed in finding at least plausibility in another person's position, you may feel less threatened and be able either to diminish or entirely forgo a fight-or-flight response.

- Although you may remain angry and still convinced that you are right, by reconsidering the perspective of the other person you may find your dislike or even cold-blooded hatred for that person starting to dissipate—like morning mist in the sunshine.

- Even if you and the other party still are convinced that you are each right, by listening, empathizing, and temporarily adopting the other's perspective you are in a good position to compromise.

When you are tolerant, your actions will almost always become more effective. By reducing the number of situations that elicit your righteous indignation, you will find your intimate acquaintances, your co-workers, and the people of your community more likely to listen to and possibly even heed what you say when you are really adamantly opposed to something. Moreover, you can focus your assertion, money, and time only on the matters most important to you.

■■■■

Antigone, the ancient Greek play by Sophocles, begins with the death of two brothers, the sons of the cursed family of King Oedipus. They have killed each other in single combat as one brother defended Thebes against an attack by the other. Their uncle, Creon, has now become tyrant ruler of that city. He is desirous of ruling with wisdom and justice. Creon therefore orders full funeral rites for the defender of Thebes but decrees that the other brother is to be left unburied and unmourned, as he had attacked the city. Anyone breaking this decree is to be killed, a seemingly justifiable position under the circumstances.

A sister, Antigone, buries her brother in defiance of Creon's order. From her perspective, by saving her brother the ignominy of having his corpse devoured by vultures and dogs, she is obeying the higher laws of the gods. Thebes officials arrest her for her civil disobedience. Creon orders her killed, despite her betrothal to his son. Again, Creon remains justified in his anger, for he accepts no other perspective than his own as ruler of Thebes.

Creon's son then brings another perspective to bear on Antigone's case and argues with his father for clemency for his bride-to-be because of the extenuating circumstances. In addition, he gives his father the new information that none of the people of Thebes want her killed, although they are afraid to say this to Creon. ". . . The city mourns for this young girl/ 'No woman,' they say, 'ever deserved death less,/ and such a brutal death for such a glorious action.' "

Creon could have first openly listened to his son, then empathized with the perspective of Antigone and the other people of Thebes and finally tolerated the difference between their perspective and his own. This would have enabled him to grant her clemency. In words that presage what hostility research has taught, his son advised such a course of action:

> . . . Now don't, please
> be quite so single-minded, self-involved,
> or assume the world is wrong and you are right.
> Whoever thinks that he alone possesses intelligence,
> the gift of eloquence, he and no one else,
> and character too . . . such men, I tell you,
> spread them open—you will find them empty. No,

it's no disgrace for a man, even a wise man,
to learn many things and not to be too rigid.
You've seen trees by a raging winter torrent,
now many sway with the flood and salvage every twig,
but not the stubborn—they're ripped out, roots and all.
Bend or break. The same when a man is sailing:
haul your sheets too taut, never give an inch,
you'll capsize, to the rest of the voyage
keel up and the rowing-benches under.

Oh give way. Relax your anger—change!
I'm young, I know, but let me offer this:
it would be best by far, I admit,
if a man were born infallible, right by nature.
If not—and things don't often go that way,
it's best to learn from those with good advice.

Instead of heeding the plea of his son, Creon is further angered by his message. As punishment, Creon heartlessly orders that Antigone be brought from the cave where she has been banished to starve to death and killed before his son, who flees with threats of revenge.

A prophet warns Creon of impending doom on Creon's house if Antigone is not forgiven and her disgraced brother properly buried. As this prophet has always proved correct in the past, Creon decides that it would be wise to take his advice. He rushes to the cave, but Antigone has already hanged herself. Creon's son then spits upon his father and misses when he lunges at him with drawn sword. The son commits suicide as Creon rushes from the cave. Creon's wife, upon hearing the sad news about her son, also commits suicide.

Creon returns to Thebes with his son's body to learn that his wife is also dead. With all he holds dear perished, he has himself led out of the city into exile. Being rigidly right without allowing Antigone and the people of Thebes a different perspective has cost him everything.

Closer to the present, we have found tolerance the best strategy to use when trying to calm our reaction to our son Lloyd's "housekeeping" standards, which all too often fall short of ours.

During a tour of plantation houses in Louisiana two years ago, we were delighted by the frequent presence of "young gentlemen's houses" set some distance from the main house. The tour guides described these small dependencies as the place young men were sent to live when they reached a certain age.

Our ability to be more tolerant of Lloyd's messy room grew when we realized that even a hundred years ago in Louisiana, parents were struggling to cope with their sons' housekeeping habits.

Intolerance isn't limited to ancient Greece. In workshops, if we ask "Against which groups and individuals are you prejudiced?," participants are likely to respond with a look of disdain and indignation. Surely we aren't suggesting that they are intolerant!

Rephrase the question to ask "What individuals or groups do you dislike?" and the response is much livelier.

> The religious right
> Senator Jesse Helms
> Self-righteous heterosexuals
> Moralists

And so on. If workshop participants came from different backgrounds, we can imagine a different round of responses.

> Atheists
> Senator Ted Kennedy
> Queers
> Homebreakers

And so on.

This exercise is useful in that people are forced, sometimes for the first time, to see not their political and religious enemies but *themselves* as intolerant. Sharing dislikes is only the first step of the workshop exercise, of course. As a next step, other members of the group are invited to share with the originator some considerations that may help him or her to empathize and eventually even to reduce the dislike he or she feels.

For example: "Try to imagine yourself as a true believer, who feels you have heard God's genuine message. You genuinely feel that unless the country as a whole repents, all of us—you, us, and all of your and our children—are doomed. If you truly felt this way, wouldn't you do everything within your power to save us all?"

Or "Try to imagine yourself as someone who has listened as

sincerely as possible to an inner voice and has never experienced any feelings of faith. You feel that believers are wrong. If you truly felt this way, would you want other believers making decisions for you?"

Participants in this workshop exercise often are not able to take all steps necessary to overcome their feelings of dislike. Often they can take the initial step of softening the intensity of their antipathies.

THE ABCS OF BEING TOLERANT

A. Every time you conclude that anger is justified, single out for additional examination any incident in which the person or group you are angry at should or ought to behave differently to be at all acceptable to you.

B. Carefully reconsider *from the perspective of the other party* whether the "misbehaving" is malicious. Also ask whether the different position is reasonable *from the perspective of the other party.*

C. Whenever possible, allow the other person to have a perspective different from your own. Accept him or her.

EXERCISES

1. Think about any important person in your life who annoys you by his or her lack of ambition, ineptitude, inappropriate level of sex drive, insensitivity, bad manners, ingratitude, or whatever. Genuinely try to see this person's actions from his or her perspective. Try to reexamine the characteristics that annoy you from this different perspective. If possible, accept that person as he or she presently is.

2. We bet that at least one of the groups listed below arouses your intolerance!

    A. Identify all groups you dislike.

- Women who wrap themselves in Saran Wrap

                or

- Women who wrap themselves in rhetoric
- Citizens who burn their flag

or

- Politicans who wrap the flag around themselves for goals of self-aggrandizement

- Artists who create obscene art

or

- Museum directors who allow the display of obscene art

or

- Politicians who want to cut off grants to museums that display obscene art

- Lawyers, dentists, doctors, businessmen, and stock-brokers who earn too much money

or

- Lazy welfare recipients who earn too little money

- Communists

or

- Reactionary rednecks

- Fundamentalists

or

- Atheists

or

- Agnostics

- And, finally, people who are apathetic!

B. Genuinely try in turn to see each group you checked as they see themselves. Try to understand their stances from their perspectives.

C. The stances of each of these groups represent their deeply and sincerely held perspectives. Do their beliefs make these people evil or malevolent? Spend a while pondering how all segments of the political and religious spectrum can feel hostility toward people different from themselves. The so-called liberal may be just as intolerant of someone he or she calls a redneck as the so-called redneck may be against different racial, ethnic, or religious groups.

D. Make a note of any group in the list whose positions are antithetical to the core of your own beliefs. Obviously you may not want to practice tolerance in extreme cases. But surely this can't apply to every group you have checked! In all the other cases, at least consider accepting the group of people with these beliefs as they are, not as you would like them to be.

CHAPTER 15

Forgive

"He who has a thousand friends has not a friend to spare.
He who has even one enemy will meet him everywhere."
>Ali Ibn-Abi-Talib, fourth successor to Muhammad,
seventh century

"Forgiveness is better than revenge."
>Pittacus when he set Alcaeus free,
after having him in his power (c. 600 B.C.)

Reprinted with special permission of King Features Syndicate

GENERAL PRINCIPLES

When to Use This Strategy

There will be times when someone—from unseen to intimate enemies—has truly wronged you, but there is little likelihood that anything you can do will have any impact on what was done or change the future. This is most often a situation in which you decide that assertion is not going to help—certainly not with someone in a car ahead who cuts you off, and probably not with a family member who did something that truly hurt you. The event is in the past. Yet you still relive it in your thoughts, still feel the hurt, the heartache, the outrage, the resentment, still experience the urge to lash out, even though in your rational mind you know that nothing will undo what happened or change the consequences. At such times *you* can release your anger by forgiving the person who wronged you.

How to Use This Strategy

Consciously decide that the person did wrong you, but that you now *choose* to forgive him or her. Acknowledge that you're wiping out the debt. It doesn't mean you have to forget what was done or not be on your guard—simply that you forgive the person for this specific transgression. Remember, you are not being forced to do it but are making a conscious choice to forgive of your own free will. Think of it as an act of grace on your part.

We recommend that you start your practice of this forgiveness strategy with relatively minor wrongs, such as bad haircuts, reports with typing errors, burned food, and spilled milk.

Some wrongs are so hurtful or devastating that your choice to forgive may not be enough to defuse your anger or anguish. Large-scale grievances—a spouse who deserted you; an alcoholic parent; or a parent who humiliated you, intimidated you, treated you like an object, or brutally beat you—probably will require help from a counselor.

You may be able to plaster over grievances of this magnitude, but eventually you will need to work through your feelings in a controlled and safe environment so that you can proceed to forgive genuinely.

Why This Strategy Works

Solid evidence that forgiveness is health enhancing is hard to identify. Noting first that there is essentially no scientific literature on this topic, Redford's good friend and colleague, Bert Kaplan, a sociologist, describes his surprise at the frequency with which the patients in Dr. Meyer Friedman's Recurrent Coronary Prevention Project cited the importance that "learning to be more forgiving" played in their learning to be less Type A.

Richard Fitzgibbons, a psychiatrist, has also written of his experience with patients who seem better able to let go of anger and the need for retribution once they are able to forgive someone who has wronged them.

Forgiveness has deep religious as well as psychological roots. In the most familiar prayer of Christians, the supplicant entreats,

"Forgive us our trespasses, as we forgive those who trespass against us." Classical Buddhism sidesteps most resentments by focusing completely on the present moment. For such Buddhists the past has no present reality. As a result everything that happened in the past, including the misbehaviors of others, becomes irrelevant *if we can let go.*

━━━

Let's take a situation in which forgiveness is extremely difficult but essential: divorce and its aftermath. More than fifteen years ago, Judith Wallerstein, a San Francisco psychologist, began her research on divorcing couples and their children. Since then she has closely followed 60 white middle-class families with 131 children, interviewing family members 1, 5, 10, and 15 years after separation. In addition, since the early 1980s her Center for the Family in Transition has counseled more than two thousand troubled families. From these vantage points, she has witnessed intense feelings of anger in the many spouses who cannot forgive their former partners.

Wallerstein reports that she has "yet to meet one man, woman, or child who emotionally accepted 'no fault' divorce." In their hearts the people she has counseled "believe in fault and in the loss associated with the decision to end the marriage." Former spouses almost inevitably blamed each other, but rarely themselves.

Among the couples in Wallerstein's research sample, half of the women and a third of the men are still intensely angry at their former spouses at least *ten years* after separating. She reports:

> In talking with many people ten years after divorce, I sometimes get the feeling I have wandered into the same play, where the same characters are using the same lines to tell the same story with the same intensity of feeling to the same audience. They do not seem to remember telling me—the audience—the same stories many times before. They do not seem to care about audience reaction.

Because the parents' feelings have not changed, anger becomes an ongoing and sometimes dominant presence in their children's lives as well. Wallerstein likens the depth of feeling among the divorcing spouses she studied to the Greek myth of Medea. When spurned by her husband for a younger woman, Medea, who dearly loves her children, murders them for revenge. "The myth captures the powerful feelings that many people have at the time of divorce, specifically the kind of anger that does not change over time and that is based on a sense of being profoundly hurt, rejected, abandoned, betrayed and outraged to the core of one's being."

In these intense expressions of anger, children can be coopted as battle allies in and out of the courtroom. Not surprising, children and adults who play these games are psychologically less stable than those who do not.

In Wallerstein's experience, children frequently blame themselves for failing to keep their parents together and their parents for getting divorced. To Wallerstein, one of the tasks of divorce for the offspring is to work through their anger at the parents and eventually to forgive them.

Clearly, for many divorced persons and their children, long-term anger with no forgiveness is deadly.

THE ABCS OF FORGIVING

A. Beginning with small matters, recognize when an injustice done to you, however wrong the person who did it was, cannot be changed or undone by anything you can do in the here and now. Realizing this, reflect on the harm the continuing anger and resentment, however well justified it may be, is doing.

B. With this knowledge in hand, make a "policy decision" to forgive the transgression—the goal being to let go the resentment and anger and get on with your life.

C. Over time, try to extend your forgiveness to situations where you have more difficulty. Continue to escalate it to ever-more-important situations. However, if you have a major grievance from your past, seek professional guidance to help you discover and work through your negative feelings.

EXERCISES

1. Imagine forgiveness in the following situations.

> **A.** You arrive home from the store and open your packages. One of the items you bought is missing, so you now must return to the store to retrieve the missing purchase.

B. The center of the lasagna your partner just served you isn't fully hot.

C. You are now late for an important meeting. You were behind a slow car you could not pass. The driver of that car sped up for the short straight expanses of road and slowed down when the road became impassable. That trip is now behind you, and you know you will be more effective in this meeting if you can get over being upset.

D. You are at a holiday gathering. A relative you have resented for years is also there. That relative has begun again to annoy you.

E. Someone of a nationality you dislike is at the same gathering as you. It will be necessary for you to interact with that person.

2. Read over your Hostility Log for incidents in which you still have not forgiven the other person(s) involved. Make an effort to practice forgiveness now.

CHAPTER 16

Have a Confidant

"No doctor can surpass a trusty friend."
Cato (?),
second-century B.C. Roman patriot

GENERAL PRINCIPLES

When to Use This Strategy

All of us should cultivate at least one intimate relationship. This confidant can be your spouse or a best friend. You should reach such a point of closeness with this person that you can telephone him or her without any special purpose, without feeling that you are wasting each other's time. You should be comfortable relying on this person whenever you need emotional or physical help, and vice-versa.

How to Use This Strategy

If you are married, devote time and energy to making the partnership as mutually enjoyable and supportive as possible for both you and your mate. If you aren't married—and even if you are—a best friend can also provide you with the needed strong and intimate social support.

For a friendship to develop the needed heartfelt intimacy, you must set aside time to be together so that the bonds between you can strengthen and deepen. If you often pass more than one day without spending time with your confidant, you need to make more of an effort to build the relationship.

If your schedule is the problem, reorder your priorities for the sake of your health and well-being. Restructure your life to see this person more often. If your confidant's schedule is the reason you are not together more often, invite him or her to share specific activities with you. If you succeed in spending more time together, congratulate yourself for asking for and getting what you need. If the other person cannot make more time available for you, seek an additional confidant who is more accessible.

How you work on your relationship with your confidant is extremely personal, as we have discovered working together on this chapter. Virginia is interested, down to every loving detail, in how people cultivate deep friendships. Redford finds even the previous paragraph gratuitous and syrupy. Whatever your own approach, get a confidant, spend a lot of time with that person, and cultivate in your own way a meaningful friendship.

When you are with your confidant, be sure to use your listening skills.

Once the bonds of mutual support with your confidant begin to deepen, try sharing with this person more and more of yourself. What are you afraid of? What makes you feel extremely comfortable? What do you dislike? What are your special likes as well? What are the worst experiences you ever had? The best? What are your small and big secret wishes for your life in the future? What are the contents of your dreams?

Most difficult will be trusting this person to still love you and take care of you when he or she knows you this intimately. You always face the possibility of rejection or betrayal. But the rewards are even greater. Once you are ready, take the risk.

Why This Strategy Works

A confidant can give you practical support, of course—a ride to the doctor's office, a respite from child care so that you can run an errand. Having a confidant has intangible benefits as well. High self-esteem is known to be health enhancing, and intimate friendships help us to feel good about ourselves. "We against the world" beats "I against the world."

On important issues, your confidant can be a helpful sounding board on effective options. He or she will likely have a more objective perspective than you.

A special friend can comfort you as no one else can when you feel heartsick or heartsore.

Research corroborates the health benefits of confiding in another person. James Pennebaker, a psychologist, studied surviving spouses in the year following an accidental death or suicide. Surprising, how well the survivor coped depended not on how the partner died but on how much in the ensuing year the surviving spouse talked with someone else about his or her thoughts and feelings.

In a study of college students enrolled in an introductory psychology course, Pennebaker asked them to write about particularly upsetting traumas in their lives. Compared with a control group, these students over the following four months visited student-health services less frequently.

Pennebaker also interviewed Holocaust survivors. Those individuals who exhibited biological signs of increased inhibition and tension when they discussed the Holocaust were more likely to visit a physician for illness in the year after the interview than before.

Exactly why sharing or even just writing down our innermost thoughts and feelings is beneficial is only partly known. Pennebaker speculates that inhibitions in sharing concerns might affect immune function, the cardiovascular system, and biochemical workings of the brain. Also, particularly upsetting traumas that are not discussed may be stored in the brain in nonlanguage form. By translating an experience into language, we may alter the way it is represented and understood in our minds.

Nineteen survivors of the Nazi concentration camps were intensively interviewed by a psychiatrist, Joel Dimsdale, in the early 1970s. Identifying themselves as part of a group was one of the major ways these people had coped with their horrible situation. This enabled them to get information, advice, and protection. Being in a group also helped reinforce a sense of individual worth. The groups these survivors belonged to ranged from political to national to family groups. The size of the group was not of key importance; simple friendship between two people was very common and was extremely effective in alleviating stress. According to the prisoners who did survive, those who weren't able to affiliate themselves in some way within a few days of internment had very limited chances of survival. Listen to the words of Sarah, one of the Holocaust survivors interviewed by Dimsdale:

> We had a group in Auschwitz singing operas and shows. We were not always in the mood for it, but sometimes in a quiet moment we would talk about the past

and everyone would play a part from a show he had seen. In Auschwitz all the time the ovens were going, day and night, and they told us they would burn us. But my sister and I consoled each other.

The evidence from science, history, and literature converges toward one conclusion: Deep friendships help us to survive, give life meaning, and bring out the best that is within us. We added this chapter on confidants to a late draft of the manuscript as a result of Redford's recent follow-up studies showing the health benefits of a confidant for heart patients seen at Duke Medical Center. (See chapter 2.)

Huckleberry Finn, one of the great characters in American literature, lacks much of a family. His drunken, no-good father is interested in him only because of the box of gold Huck found in a robber's cave. Huck does have two wonderful friends in his pal Tom Sawyer and Jim, the runaway slave whom he takes up with.

Jim and Huck become confidants while they are drifting down the Mississippi River on a raft as they both run away. When Jim is captured and held by bounty seekers, Huck is faced with a moral quandary over whether he should contact Jim's former owner or not, the latter course a sin Huck thinks will condemn him to hell. At first Huck pens a note to the former owner, but then he begins to muse:

> [I] laid the paper down and set there thinking—thinking how good it was all this happened so, and how near I come to being lost and going to hell. And went on thinking. And got to thinking over our trip down the river; and I see Jim before me, all the time, in the day, and in the nighttime, sometimes moonlight, sometimes storms, and we afloating along, talking, and singing, and laughing. But somehow I couldn't seem to strike no places to harden me against him, but only the other kind. I'd see him standing my watch on top of his'n, stead of calling me, so I could go on sleeping; and see him how glad he was when I come back out of the fog; and when I come to him again in the swamp, up there where the feud was; and such-like times; and would always call me honey, and pet me, and do everything he could think of

for me, and how good he always was; and at last I struck the time I saved him by telling the men we had small-pox aboard, and he was so grateful, and said I was the best friend old Jim ever had in the world, and the *only* one he's got now; and then I happened to look around, and see that paper.

It was a close place. I took it up, and held it in my hand. I was a trembling, because I'd got to decide, forever, betwixt two things, and I knowed it. I studied a minute, sort of holding my breath, and then says to myself:

"All right, then, I'll *go* to hell"—and then tore it up.

It was awful thoughts, and awful words, but they was said. And I let them stay said; and never thought no more about reforming. I shoved the whole thing out of my head; and said I would take up wickedness again, which was in my line, being brung up to it, and the other warn't. And for a starter, I would go to work and steal Jim out of slavery again. . . .

Whether having Jim as a confidant helped Huck to live longer we obviously can't say. Jim's goodness, loyalty, and kindness had counted for enough to enable Huck to transcend the values of his society and to live better.

THE ABCS OF HAVING A CONFIDANT

A. Determine if you already have a close relationship with someone. If the answer is yes, cultivate that relationship. If the answer is no, select a suitable person and work on forging closer ties between the two of you.

B. Monitor whether you are spending enough time with this person to deepen your relationship. If the problem is your schedule, allot more time. If the problem is the schedule of the other person, see if he or she can spend more time with you. If this is impossible, get an additional confidant.

C. Gradually begin to share inner thoughts and feelings as well as services, goods, and time spent together.

EXERCISES

1. Think about any best friends you had in the past. If you know their whereabouts, telephone just to say hello. If calling is too expensive, drop them a note.

2. Whether you already have a satisfactory confidant or not, make a list of people you like and make a conscious decision to develop friendships with them.

STRATEGIES TO HELP YOU
ADOPT POSITIVE ATTITUDES

In these final few chapters, we will complete our change of perspective, to focus now on positive matters of the heart. We began with learning strategies focused on reason (chapter 3) and deflection (chapters 4, 5, and 6) to control hostile urges, feelings, and thoughts. When you apply these strategies, you overcome negative feelings or sidestep a problem. Assertion (chapter 8) also focuses on correcting a problem that already exists.

With the section on improving relationships, your focus shifted. Listening (chapter 10), trusting (chapter 11), empathizing (chapter 13), tolerating (chapter 14), and forgiving (chapter 15) can be means of overcoming problems with others. But all of these skills except forgiveness also can be used to establish good relations even when no problem exists. Caring for pets (chapter 9), performing community service (chapter 12), and developing confidants (chapter 16) also focus on building good relations with others.

The survival skills in chapters 17, 18, and 19 go further and are, perhaps, the most heart-healthy of all the strategies presented. Although you can—and should—use humor ("Laugh at Yourself," chapter 17) as an excellent deflecting strategy, you can also entertain yourself and others with humor, for heartfelt pleasure.

We all live by some set of values, even though we may give them little thought. Joining a religious community with like-minded values ("Become More Religious," chapter 18) will provide you with formal opportunities to reflect upon what you want to value. With the support of like-minded individuals in the congregation, you will also be encouraged to put your heart and soul into your life. In addition, this same congregation can potentially be a source of a confidant.

Living each day as fully as possible becomes easier once you focus on the present (chapter 19).

So far in this book, we've learned the skills necessary to do the hard work of controlling hostility for a lifetime. This is certainly all to the good. Now in the chapters ahead are some strategies to help you maximize these gains and garner some additional benefits.

A life of all work, no play, and little thoughtfulness is an incomplete, faint-hearted existence. Your life can be better than that. So for the next three chapters, relax and enjoy yourself.

CHAPTER 17

Laugh at Yourself

"A cheerful heart is a good medicine, but a downcast spirit dries up the bones."   Proverbs 17:22

"You grow up the day you have the first real laugh—at yourself."   Ethel Barrymore,
                    twentieth-century U.S. actress

GENERAL PRINCIPLES

When to Use This Strategy

Suppose the Hostility Roadmap leads you to conclude that your hostility is either petty, unjustified, or that you have no effective response. In addition to those deflection strategies we described in chapters 4, 5, and 6, there is another strategy that will actually convert your negative emotions to a positive emotion: the use of humor.

Not all forms of humor fit our purpose here. When hostile people do engage in humor, it is most often negative and attacking—ridicule. The hostile person will laugh at the expense of someone else's failings, which, after all, is just as much an aggressive as a humorous activity.

Bedroom and bathroom humor, as well as anti-religious jokes, which generally arise from embarrassment or fear, and jokes directed at the ethnics, the disabled, one or the other gender, and specific racial groups, which ultimately belittle a whole category of people, all qualify as negative mirth-making. This isn't the heart-healthy humor we urge you to cultivate.

Try instead to make *your own* foibles or the circumstances that are temporarily overwhelming you the object of your humor. If you find yourself in a compromised position, try making fun of your own sense of self-importance and your own ridiculousness. If the problem involves others only, try to perceive as humorous potentially annoying people and circumstances we all encounter many times a day. Seeing the humorous side of a dreary situation can help you escape your self-imposed boundaries and problem.

Given that so much of our anger is either petty, unjustified, or useless (since there's no effective response available), we hostile people miss countless opportunities to enjoy a laugh at our own expense. Notice that we said *"enjoy* a laugh"—laughter *is* pleasurable, a positive emotion. As such, it is a very effective antidote to all those *negative* emotions—anger, irritation, resentment, frustration, annoyance, pique, outrage, fury, and so on—that make up so much of the daily experience of hostile people everywhere.

How to Use This Strategy

Having begun to master some of the other strategies and assessment techniques described in earlier chapters, you have now become more adept at recognizing those situations in which your hostility is either petty, unjustified, or useless. Seeing the futility of your anger, you are in a position to make fun of it by using a variety of humor-inducing devices.

Laugh at your own self-importance by *catastrophizing* about any situation you have already turned into a big deal. Apply your ability to conduct a dialogue with yourself to spin some of your unjustified annoyances at other people to a ridiculous extreme. As you find yourself beginning to dislike the elderly woman at the head of the bank line who seems to be transacting a lifetime of financial arrangements, make fun of your own perspective that the business of the bank should revolve around you.

> "Yeah, these little old ladies are really sneaky. They have an organization that gives them a list of people who have to come down here to the bank every day and then they lie in wait outside, and when they see us coming they slip into the line just ahead of us. Not too far ahead, mind you, they want to make sure we see 'em so we can start to stew before they even get to do their number. And then when they get up to the teller, they really swing into *in*action! 'Oh my, I don't seem to have my deposit slip filled out right!' they whine. Oh boy, she's gonna get the teller to have to look up her number in the computer—I might as well take a nap! I bet they get a commission for every person they keep waiting behind them in the line for more than ten minutes!"

Don't hold back. Let your sense of persecution carry you away. Spin out to extremes the evil intent on the part of that really sweet-looking elderly woman ahead of you in line. Before you finish, we bet there will be at least the hint of a smile playing about your lips. And the cynical thoughts, angry feelings, and urge to do something will have receded into the oblivion where they belong.

Another way to catastrophize is to turn annoying circumstances into happenings of world importance, once again carrying your sense of self-importance to an extreme. Suppose you find yourself infuriated that your final exam (or major presentation at work) falls on your birthday:

> "I must be a *very* important person to have the entire school's exam schedule arranged around my birthday. I wonder how much the other students will pay me to switch my birthday to April!"

Another useful form of humor you might apply is *irony*. Make fun of a situation by describing it as the opposite of what it really is. For example, when in a bank line, you might reply to someone who asks you if the line is moving fast, "Well, it was until I got into it." Or try "This line is faster than a rolling O. Can you fill out your bank slip within forty-five minutes?" In the first example, by stating that you actually have the power to make a line stop moving, you call attention, not only in your own mind but in the other person's as well, to the silliness of taking personally slow-moving lines. In the second example, you are choosing to laugh.

If irony doesn't feel right, consider *slapstick*. Put imaginary silly hats on everyone in front of you in the bank line. If you prefer, imagine them once you've fed them jumping beans. The quiet little man near the front of the line may begin to dance the cha-cha.

You may not be into hats or jumping beans. How about *puns* or *double entendres*? Think, "I've got it! The woman in the front of the line who has just described every intimate detail of her entire financial history to the teller thinks that 'express' line is short for *expression*. She certainly can express herself in great detail. No wonder she chose the express line!"

How about hooking together *a silly combination* of people, ideas, or behaviors? In turn, choose the most staid and the wildest-looking persons in the entire line. Now imagine the wildest as the teller announcing to the most staid that the bank's board has been really listening to his investment ideas recently!

Exaggeration is frequently involved in humor.

> "I'd rather sit on a bed of nails than stand in this bank line."

Play with your initial exaggeration.

> "I'd rather sit on a bed of nails with an elephant on top of me than stand in this bank line."

Keep asking yourself what else could embroider your initial exaggeration. Soon you'll have reached the teller.

Anticipate situations or individuals likely to rile or stress you in the future. Dwight David Eisenhower reportedly overcame nervousness about speaking in public with a little trick of transferring his nervousness to his audience: "I look out at all the people in the audience and just imagine that everyone out there is sitting in his tattered old underwear."

Make a list of anticipated negative encounters with powerful and disliked persons whose behaviors you cannot change. Muse for each case whether a humorous image of that person would defuse the situation. Create such images now and hold them in reserve until they are needed.

Whatever form of humor you adopt, invest in it the energy you formerly spent fuming. Basically, the goal of the humor strategy is to turn your frowns of irritation into smiles of whimsy, or even belly laughs.

Why This Strategy Works

First of all, by actually seeing the humor in a bad situation and laughing at yourself, you will force anger, and the harmful physiological effects that go with it, from your brain and body. Anger and humor cannot be in the same mind at the same time!

In *Anatomy of an Illness,* Norman Cousins championed the idea that humor is restorative by describing his own use of old "Candid Camera" episodes and Marx Brothers films as well as humor books, especially E. B. and Katherine White's *Subtreasury of American Humor* and Max Eastman's *The Enjoyment of Laughter.* Cousins' maintained humor, along with his own will to live, and, purportedly, vitamin C, helped him to overcome what appears to have been a potentially fatal collagen disease. Whether you accept this anecdotal evidence or not, his example and writings have stimulated scientific research into the biology of humor, and what we are learning so far suggests that humor is healthful.

Numerous laboratory experiments lead to the conclusion that amusing a subject sharply reduces the likelihood that he or she will subsequently engage in overt acts of aggression.

Studies of the physiology of humor also suggest its healthfulness. At first, it is correlated to increased heart rate, increased skin conductance of electric currents, and altered respiration, with deeper and faster breathing, including more prolonged breathing out than breathing in. Experiencing something or someone as funny and laughing at it will arouse you. But eventually you calm down, and sometimes your body becomes calmer than before you laughed in the first place.

This calming effect of positive emotions was clearly shown in a study by Barbara Fredrickson and Robert Levenson, University of California psychologists. All subjects first viewed a frightening film of a man inching along the ledge of a tall building, falling, barely grabbing the ledge and hanging on—all the while struggling to keep from dropping. Everyone reported increased fear after this film. Next, some subjects watched a film of a puppy playing with a flower that all rated as amusing; others watched a contentment-inducing film of waves breaking; others watched a sad film of a son crying as his father is dying; and others watched an emotionally neutral film of colored sticks piling up.

Not surprising, everyone showed an increase in heart rate and a constriction of skin blood vessels after viewing the fear-inducing film. Compared with those who next viewed the neutral film, those subjects who viewed the amusing puppy film showed a more rapid recovery of cardiovascular arousal to the baseline levels measured at the start of the study.

This is one of the first studies to so clearly document the potential physiological benefits to be gained from the experiencing of positive emotions like amusement. It helps bring into the realm of scientific discourse the old saying that "laughter is the best medicine."

Although hostile people may have difficulty taking humor seriously, it can be very helpful to them. As reported by her psychotherapist, a twenty-two-year-old woman with a husband and a three-year-old son was experiencing great difficulty with her hostility. She reported screaming at and berating her husband, and even occasionally throwing things at him. She would scream at her three-year-old son at the top of her voice. She jumped up and down, smashed things, and once physically attacked the child. She had contemplated suicide because her violent temper "makes everyone, including me, miserable." At first her psychotherapist tried deep muscular relaxation. He attempted to reintroduce her in a calm, professional setting to the scenes that had made her angry, with the goal of desensitizing her. That was not successful. What did succeed was when he presented the scenes of situations that usually upset her as slapstick comedy.

> As you're driving to the supermarket, little Pascal the Rascal begins to get restless. Suddenly he drops from his position on the ceiling and trampolines off the rear seat onto the rearview mirror. From this precarious position, he amuses himself by flashing obscene hand gestures at shocked pedestrians. As you begin to turn in to the supermarket parking lot, Pascal alights from his perch and lands with both feet on the accelerator. As the car careens through the parking lot, you hear Pascal observe, "Hmm, twenty-five to eighty in two seconds— not bad." But right now your main concern are the two

elderly and matronly women whom you're bearing down upon. You can see them very clearly, limping toward the door of the supermarket clutching their little bargain coupons. One, who is clutching a prayerbook in her other hand, turns and, upon seeing a car approaching her at 70 mph, utters a string of profanities, throws her coupons in the air, and lays a strip of Neolite as she sprints out of the way and does a swan dive into a nearby open manhole. The other, moving equally fast, nimbly eludes your car and takes refuge in a nearby shopping cart, which picks up speed as it rolls downhill across the parking lot with Robert Ironside in hot pursuit.

With her therapist helping her to focus on the humorous aspect of scenes that made her angry, the patient after eight sessions was back in control. She reported major reductions in the frequency and intensity of her angry responses to interactions with her son and husband. Other relatives noted the improvement in her temper. Her son's behavior improved as well. As corroboration, a new round of psychological tests administered after humor therapy showed she was less impulsive, resentful, angry, and tense. Physiological measures also showed that her health had improved.

━━━━

According to the humorist Roger Rosenblatt, his mother is one of the funniest people he knows, capable of producing everlasting humor that saves herself as well as others. She and other true humorists are giving, companionable, full of character, yet still serious. They draw you in, at least close enough to say who they are. They give you power over your menaces. Rosenblatt illustrates what he means by describing a luncheon outing with his then-elderly mother. He commented to her and his wife that they were having a nice time.

"Yes," said his mother. "But the next time we go out, we ought to invite Joseph Cotten." His wife and he searched each other's eyes for an explanation.

"Why, Ma?" he asked.

"Because," said his mother, "Joseph Cotten can tell exactly what part of the country you came from by your dialect."

"Ma," he said, after guessing whom she was thinking of, "do

you mean Rex Harrison or Leslie Howard, when they played Professor Higgins? *He* could identify everyone's dialect."

His mother rummaged through her muddle. She hated her confusion, and she could see how unhappy it made them.

"Oh, yes. You're right," she said, and paused a perfect Jack Benny pause. "But since we've already invited Joseph Cotten, I don't think it would be right to renege."

They all laughed a very long time.

Virginia lacks patience with or talent for filling out forms. She so hurriedly filled out a recent car registration renewal application that she failed to list our insurance carrier. The Department of Motor Vehicles returned the form with her check, asking for the additional information. When Redford saw the letter with the returned application lying on the kitchen counter, he became upset. With only two weeks remaining on the old registration, he immediately envisioned all sorts of terrible outcomes. He concluded that because Virginia had made the mistake, she should take care of the matter by taking the completed form and check to the local office of the Department of Motor Vehicles, a visit that inevitably involves a long wait, no matter which line you choose.

Virginia said she would mail the materials in again. Two weeks was plenty of time for a letter to make it to the state capital, twenty-five miles away. Furthermore, she didn't appreciate being yelled at.

Redford tried to inject some catastrophizing humor by painting a bleak scene of the application not getting there and the dire consequences that would result—expired registration, invalidated insurance, accident with us at fault, lawsuit, loss of home and all our savings! Virginia rejoined with more than a hint of annoyance in her voice that she considered his concern inappropriate. She was prepared to mail in the application. If he wanted it hand delivered, that was his problem, and he would have to take it himself.

Redford replied with considerable agitation that he'd do just that, and there at the time is where the unpleasant episode ended. He soaked for a long time in the tub, and she went to sleep before he got out.

Two weeks later, the day of the deadline, Redford still had the unmailed application. He planned to take it that day but remembered he had a tight schedule, with a morning flight out of town.

Virginia said, rubbing it in, that as an act of generosity she'd take the stupid form in.

By now, both Redford and Virginia saw the incident more as fodder for *Anger Kills* than a crisis. Over the next few months, whenever he was giving a talk, Redford used his catastrophizing about the registration application to illustrate the use of humor to counter hostility.

Here several points are worth making. First, despite a professional interest in the subject and knowledge about the harm angry outbursts wreak on your body, plus years of practice with anger control, both Redford and Virginia lost their tempers initially. Neither found the occasion at all funny, despite Redford's attempt at catastrophizing.

You won't always be able to see the humor in a situation either, no matter how much you want to. Still, give it a try whenever humor is appropriate. You will delay more harmful reactions, and sometimes you will succeed in defusing your unhealthy angry feelings. Your success rate will improve with practice.

In the car registration incident, perhaps neither of us used humor soon enough to prevent the initial angry outbursts and unpleasant interchanges. Reliving the event, which we can now do humorously, still has been beneficial. Every time Redford retells the story and laughs at his own catastrophizing, he reinforces to himself the silliness of his initial reaction. Rather than reexperiencing his anger, he uses all these occasions of reliving the car registration incident as practice for the next time Virginia messes something up.

As a result, the next time Virginia fills out a form incorrectly, Redford may be able to find his initial catastrophizing funny, and he'll be able to defuse his anger.

The lesson: Get hostility under control right away. If not, practice and practice again, with your goal of reducing hostility ever in mind. Like Redford, you won't always initially succeed, but your batting average will improve greatly, as Virginia can attest.

THE ABCS OF USING HUMOR

A. Noting the pettiness, unreasonableness, or uselessness of your hostile thoughts, feelings, or urges in a given situation, decide to make fun of yourself for having gotten into such a state over something so trivial and unreasonable.   .

B. Try one or more techniques to make yourself smile or possibly even snicker:

- You can catastrophize, exaggerating the importance of the situation and yourself. (Remember the license application.)

- You can play with your untrue impending sense of doom or your untrue sense of self-importance. (Remember the slow/fast-moving bank line.)

- By actively applying whimsy, you can substitute a new imagined reality. (Remember all those silly hats and Pascal the Rascal!)

- You can entertain yourself with puns and double entendres. (Express line, my foot!)

- You can link together improbable combinations from elements in your current situation, making both parts funny.

- You can unfavorably compare your present plight with an exaggerated undesirable situation. (Remember the bed of nails with the elephant on top.)

C. Apply humor more and more often, until instead of the hostile thoughts, feelings, and urges you formerly experienced so often you are now spending more and more of your consciousness developing the positive emotion of laughter.

EXERCISES

1. The next time you are in a traffic jam, take a good *(but discreet)* look at the driver behind you. Invent the funniest story you can about where he or she has just been. Make his or her delay of the moment have a humorous consequence.

2. Imagine yourself in the return line of a discount store after a major holiday. You are becoming irritated. Apply in turn exaggerated self-importance, irony, slapstick, puns, double entendres, and ridiculous combinations as well as exaggeration to keep from getting annoyed with the wait.

3. You are once again in the return line of that same discount store and are again becoming irritated. Invent a new means of humorously entertaining yourself without resorting to hostility. The only rules are that your invention must be harmless and at least mildly entertaining.

4. Imagine yourself resolved to apply the humor strategy on a situation in which you find yourself on an expressway with one lane closed. Traffic is inching along. Instead of taking advantage of an opening, an ancient Volkswagen ahead of you lets several other drivers break in. Imagine that the bumper sticker on the VW reads "I am driving this way to piss you off!"

5. Think about powerful, unpleasant people you cannot avoid or control. Create a funny mental image of each, in anticipation of your next encounter.

6. Throughout this book we have included cartoons that make light of the daily round of cynicism, anger, and aggression that is the lot of the hostile person. For the next few months, assemble your own collection of cartoons that both tickle your funny bone and focus on hostile matters. Conjure up these images to help stir your laughter in daily life.

CHAPTER **18**
Become More Religious

"There is no age which religion does not become."
Erasmus,
sixteenth-century Dutch scholar

GENERAL PRINCIPLES

When to Use This Strategy

Although it's not a specific response to a particular situation that provokes your hostility, joining and becoming an active participant in a religious community can be a very effective means of helping yourself to achieve a more positive philosophical outlook. This outlook will, in turn, act in many, many ways to help curb your cynicism, anger, and aggression.

How to Use This Strategy

If you don't already attend the services of some religious group—at a church, synagogue, temple, mosque, whatever—investigate one that seems compatible with your general orientation and attend a few times. (If you are uncomfortable with the formal doctrines of all religions, you might want to go to a meeting of the Ethical Culture Society.) If the services are in your neighborhood, some congregational contacts might carry over into convenient friendships. If you feel welcome, in genuine agreement with the tenets and practices of the group, and confident that your self-identity is not being compromised, go ahead and become a member. If you're already a member of a religious group, so much the better. In both cases your next step is to become a *truly practicing member,* practicing whatever is preached with all your heart.

This means first of all that you make an earnest effort to learn about the core teachings of the religious tradition of the community you have joined. We know of no major religion that at its core extols cynicism, anger, or aggression. If you perceive that, it's sadly grafted on, a result of our human weakness. You will almost certainly find your religion teaching that you should accord others the same consideration, regard, kindness, and gentleness that you would like them to accord you. This will happen because all the world's major religions have a core philosophy that is basically one version or another of the Golden Rule—do unto others as you would have them do unto you.

In his book *Theology for the Third Millenium,* the theologian Hans Kung drives home this point when he defines a "*true* and *good* religion" as one whose ". . . teachings on faith and morals, rites and institutions *support* human beings in their human identity, and allows them to gain a meaningful and fruitful existence." If you adopt a religion that has this perspective and try to make it part of your life, you will become a less hostile and a more caring person.

The full practice of any religious tradition means not only that you educate yourself in the philosophy but also that you actively participate in the organized activities of the religious community. Attend worship services regularly, pray or meditate alone and together with others, and join small groups within the larger body, like a Bible study group, singles or couples group, or a group working to help needy people in your community. This provides you with many opportunities to practice the other strategies you are already cultivating—trusting, meditation, community service, and on and on. You will have a new source of potential confidants. You also gain social connections—an extended family that you can depend on for social support—a precious commodity that hostile people seem so often to lack or even avoid.

Why This Strategy Works

Gerald Caplan, an epidemiologist, has spent his life studying support systems and community mental health. He sees religion as the most commonly used support system. When someone joins a religious group, he or she strengthens bonds with a large number of people who share a theology, value system, and body of traditions. In most groups, members are enjoined to help one another, especially in time of acute needs. During crisis times such as birth, marriage, illness, and death, members benefit from comforting service programs and religious ceremonies.

These external benefits are buttressed by the internal supports of a meaningful value system and set of guidelines for living. A religious person can draw on a larger well of wisdom when grappling with life's problems.

Your religious values aren't tied to geography, as are your job and friends. If you belong to a large denomination and have to move, you'll be welcomed in your new place.

As another benefit, the practice of prayer or meditation, integral to all religions, will help improve your own meditation skills.

Several studies suggest that being religious improves one's physical health. Researchers at Hadassah University found that Jewish residents of Jerusalem who describe themselves as secular have four times greater a risk of suffering a heart attack than residents who describe themselves as religiously orthodox. The Hadassah scientists also found higher levels of cholesterol among seventeen- to eighteen-year-old secular residents of Jerusalem than among their religiously orthodox counterparts. The differences could not be explained by dietary fat intake.

In a large-scale study in Evans County, Georgia, among citizens who reported frequent attendance at church, blood-pressure levels were lower than among those who attended church less often. In another large study in Washington County, Maryland, persons who reported attending church at least once a week were much less prone to subsequent deaths from heart disease than less frequent churchgoers. This decreased risk holds up after adjustments are made for smoking, social class, and water quality. (Of course, someone with serious heart disease might have been unable to attend church long before a fatal attack, although attempts to consider this possibility indicated that subjects' previous general coronary health was not a factor.)

Psychological studies correlating religious practices to general mental health suggest that some ways of being religious appear beneficial, others not. The differences appear to relate not to a particular creed but to how beliefs are held.

The emerging wisdom differentiates among three religious orientations:

- *Intrinsic* practitioners find the main meaning for their lives in their religion. Having embraced a creed, the individual endeavors to internalize it and to follow it fully. In most studies, this correlates with positive mental health.

- *Questers* see religion as expression of the search for meaning in the personal and social world. These "self-starters" give a number of hours to helping others. Young adults who are questers tend to have excellent mental health.

- Those who have an *extrinsic* orientation, who find religion useful but selectively shape their creed to fit their other interests, tend to be less mentally healthy.

One of the greatest Catholic philosophers of the twentieth century was not born into his faith. Jacques Maritain was reared by his divorced mother as a liberal French Protestant, but the main influence on his early life was his teachers. By his later reports, they deeply revered science and focused their studies almost exclusively on what could be measured, quantified, and proven. As a result, no attention was paid to invisible and immaterial subjects.

Jacques found this ignorance of spiritual matters intolerable, and he despaired of ever finding answers to his deepest questions about the meaning of life. This upset him enough that at sixteen years of age, he is reported to have hurled himself upon his bedroom rug in hopelessness.

Later, when he was a student at the Sorbonne, he and his girlfriend, the Jewish Russian classmate Raïssa Oumansoff, concluded that life was not worth living unless one could discover truth and the differences between goodness and evil, justice and injustice. They could accept unhappiness but not absurdity and moral nihilism.

One afternoon, while in the Jardin des Plantes, Jacques and Raïssa made a vow: If they did not discover some meaning to life before the end of the year, they would commit suicide.

A professor at the neighboring Collège de France rescued the disenchanted young couple from their despair. In his lectures, Henri Bergson emphasized the value of intuition in scientific thinking, and argued that reality is beyond rational understanding. This permission to consider matters beyond the confines of narrowly defined material considerations was a breakthrough beginning for Jacques and Raïssa.

A couple of years later and after their marriage, the Maritains embraced Catholicism.

> We ask God, although one can serve Him in every condition, to grant us the favor of being witness to His Name, and if He wills to dispense us from misery, to help us embrace a state in which we may be in His grace, not in that of a godless world, and which keeps the simplicity, the purity and the poverty of the Gospel.

This newfound orientation would guide the couple for the remainder of their lives.

Jacques and Raïssa spent the next four years after their conversion reading the lives of saints as well as spiritual and mystical writings. Greatly inspired by St. Thomas Aquinas, the medieval Catholic philosopher, Jacques set about to reconcile the authentic philosophic spirit of inquiry of his earlier schooling with his newly found faith, and in the process wrote more than fifty books.

Maritain always based his pronouncements on what he saw as the will of God. Some of his writings from all periods of his life are narrow and angry, the opposite of the attitude we recommend you adopt. When they are considered as a whole, however, Maritain's teachings usually advocated compassion and charity.

During the 1920s, Maritain focused mainly on speculative philosophy. By the 1930s, when he was already in his late forties to fifties, as the lot of the poor worsened and totalitarian regimes arose in Germany, Italy, and Spain, Maritain embraced as the will of God liberal and democratic solutions to economic and social problems. He championed the rescue of European Jews from Nazi persecution, racial equality, the dignity and rights of labor, and the alleviation of the sufferings of the poor as implications of his religious beliefs.

> To say that a man is a person is to say that in the depth of his being he is more a whole than a part and more independent than servile. It is to say that he is a minute fragment of matter that is at the same time a universe, a beggar who participates in the absolute being, mortal flesh whose value is eternal, and a bit of straw into which heaven enters. It is this metaphysical mystery that religious thought designates when it says that the person is the image of God.

Maritain's union of faith, courage, intelligence, and (usually) benevolence made him a very effective writer. In France and America, he became a source of political, social, or spiritual inspiration for many of the leading intellectuals of his generation, who saw him as a just and good man without equal.

In his medical practice, Redford has frequently encountered patients, especially men in their late twenties and early thirties, who say that their religious conversion transformed their lives. Before embracing a religion, they overindulged in alcohol, drove cars recklessly, or abused their wives and children. After conversion, particularly if they remained active participants in their religion, they cut back on alcohol, controlled their pursuit of thrills, and were kinder, gentler husbands and fathers.

We have no hesitation in advising that for many people, becoming more religious can be a very effective antidote for hostility and anger.

THE ABCS OF BECOMING MORE RELIGIOUS

A. Choose a religious community and join it with a commitment to be a truly practicing member. (If you are already a member, renew your commitment.)

B. Study the teachings of your chosen religion and learn what is really at its core. Day by day, try to put the core philosophy to work in your life.

C. Actively participate in the ongoing activities of your chosen religious community.

EXERCISES

1. Read a book on world religions. We recommend Huston Smith's *The World's Religions* (rev. ed. of *The Religions of Man*), (San Francisco: Harper Collins, 1991), which is available in paperbound and hardbound editions.

2. If you are not yet affiliated with a religious sect, attend services of different faiths in your community. (Remember to practice tolerance!) If you are already a member of a religious sect but not very active, join in a specific new activity, such as teaching in a religious education program, participating in a singles group, or becoming active in a community-service project.

CHAPTER 19

Pretend Today Is Your Last

"Look to this day!
For it is life, the very life of life
In its brief course lie all the verities
    and realities of your existence:
        The bliss of growth,
        The glory of action,
        The splendor of beauty;
        For yesterday is but a dream,
        And tomorrow is only a vision;
But today, well lived, makes every
    yesterday a dream of happiness
And every tomorrow a vision of hope.
Look well, therefore, to this day."
                    Kālidāsa (?),
                    fifth-century Indian poet and playwright

GENERAL PRINCIPLES

When to Use This Strategy

Will it take a heart attack to make you less hostile? One of the most common responses Redford hears from heart patients to his queries about anger is, "Well, now, before my heart attack I used to get angry a lot. But since then, I've decided it's better to walk away from anger."

Somehow, being brought face to face with one's own mortality has a way of focusing attention on what's really important. Therefore, when you are having difficulty practicing some of the strategies we've described in earlier chapters, wondering if it's worth the effort, we suggest you try this: *Pretend today is your last.*

Cow philosophy

How to Use This Strategy

Pretend that you have just received from your doctor the terrible news that you have a fatal illness and have only a few days or weeks to live. (Life is a fatal illness that always ends in death—the only difference between most of us and those who know they have a specific fatal illness is that we are less informed as to the amount of time remaining.)

That's it. Just pretend you've gotten the bad news.

Now see if going through a typical day viewing the world through the eyes of someone forced to confront mortal existence will make you more eager to apply the strategies in this book, particularly those that orient you more positively toward others.

As part of our workshops, we ask participants to imagine that a giant meteor is hurtling toward Earth. No physical changes will occur until the instant that the planet blows up, which is estimated to be forty-seven hours from now. The workshop assignment is to describe how you would spend those forty-seven hours.

"I'd walk in the woods. Depending on the season, I would look for wildflowers or mushrooms."

"I'd want to spend the time with my children."

"I'd make love, eat juicy steaks, and drink fine red wine."

"I would immediately get in touch with my sister. We and other friends would head for the beach."

Remarks are always in this vein. We have yet to hear anyone say they would head to the office or settle a grudge.

Life often presents us with evidence of our own finiteness, thereby forcing us to realize, without even having to pretend, that our life can end at any time. This happened recently for us when our son Lloyd got a call from the chief of the volunteer fire department to which he and some of his friends belong.

The chief was calling to see if Lloyd knew where one of his friends might be on that particular Saturday afternoon, because the friend's father had just been killed in an automobile accident. Virginia was in town at the library. After a while, Redford and Lloyd pulled themselves together as they absorbed the tragic news and prepared to pay a condolence call on the grieving family.

As we rode into town that evening, we found ourselves wondering, "What if it had been—as it so easily could have been on the slick roads of that rainy Saturday afternoon—one of us whose life had been so abruptly snuffed out? Is there anything we would regret not having done?"

Such thoughts bring home to us the importance of living each minute of each day so that when our last day does arrive there will be nothing for us to regret not having done. Chances are that if we try to live each day in this way, our hostile impulses will be easier to put aside.

Why This Strategy Works

The things you think, feel, and do today become the memories you lay down for tomorrow. If so much of your experience today consists of cynical thoughts, angry feelings, and aggressive acts, then this is what you and others will have to remember tomorrow.

On the other hand, you can spend more time relating in positive ways toward your significant other, your offspring, and everyone else, including yourself. And affirm rather than tear down everyone's basic humanity. Those affirmations will then be the memories that fill your tomorrows, thus creating for yourself a happier future and past at the same time.

You also will garner immediate benefits. By focusing on the present, you will eliminate many sources of stress and anxiety. You will also eliminate all the time you waste vaguely musing about "if only."

Admitting the importance of each minute of your limited life span is scary, but facing this reality may help you to get the most out of your brief time on Earth. You can enjoy a very fulfilling existence if you are willing to put thought and effort into how you live each minute. In chapter 4, which deals with stopping hostile thoughts, we described the concept of multimind. Your brain has been multiply programmed with all of your evolutionary heritages, so you are likely to have multiple thoughts and perspectives on most subjects. Although you have only one thought at a time, if you make the effort you can review all of your thoughts in sequence, so that you get beyond your first reaction. After that, *you* can decide which of your thoughts align with the most authentic parts of your being. Once you know what you truly think and feel, *you* can then review what options for action you have at any moment, including, if appropriate, any of your strategies from your anti-hostility arsenal. In other words, by gaining control over yourself, you can assume the roles of director and producer in your life.

Ebenezer Scrooge's miserable early life is familiar to millions of readers of Charles Dickens's *A Christmas Carol*. Scrooge had been a solitary child, neglected by his friends. He was then banished by his father to boarding school. Once he was grown, his beloved sister died prematurely. Finally, his girlfriend married another after she realized Scrooge loved money more than he loved her.

When the reader first meets Scrooge at his office on Christmas Eve, the miser is the ultimate caricature of the hostile personality. Scrooge is crotchety to his clerk, stints on heating fuel, and refuses his nephew's invitation to dinner: "Hard and sharp as flint, from which no steel had ever struck out generous fire, secret, and self-contained, and solitary as an oyster."

Some men from the neighborhood ask Scrooge to make some slight provision for the poor and destitute: "Many thousands are in want of common necessaries; hundreds of thousands are in want of common comforts, sir." He rejects this opportunity. To Scrooge, prisons, union workhouses, the treadmill, the poor law, and survival of the fittest are useful institutions. "It's not my business. . . . It's enough for a man to understand his own business, and not to interfere with other people's. Mine occupies me constantly."

Once home, Scrooge is visited by the ghost of his former partner, who now must drag around a tail of cash-boxes, keys, padlocks, ledgers, deeds, and heavy purses wrought in steel, a chain he forged in life.

Upset by the miserable spectre, Scrooge cries out, "But you were always a good man of business." " 'Business?' cried the Ghost, wringing his hands again. 'Mankind was my business. The common welfare was my business; charity, mercy, forbearance, and benevolence were all my business. The dealings of my trade were but a drop of water in the comprehensive ocean of my business!' "

The ex-partner tells Scrooge that he will be visited by the three successive ghosts of Christmases past, present, and future. With their help, Scrooge finally is forced to confront the small-mindedness of his present life and his own mortality.

Scrooge sees for the first time his own sad history, his present meanness of spirit, and his impending lonely, meaningless death—if he continues to live each present day badly. This new insight is enough to transform Scrooge into a generous man who truly lives each day as though it were his last.

That very Christmas Day, Scrooge gives away a fat turkey, spends time at his nephew's home, and makes a contribution to charity. The next day, he stokes up enough fire to heat his office well and raises the salary of his clerk.

He "became as good a friend, as good a master, and as good a man as the good old City knew, or any other good old city, town, or borough in the good old world."

Before it was too late, Scrooge had finally learned to live each day well.

So can you.

THE ABCS OF PRETENDING
TODAY IS YOUR LAST

A. Decide to spend a day acting as though it may be the last day you have to live.

B. As you approach every encounter with this view in mind, pay close attention to how it inclines you to behave.

C. At the end of the day, evaluate whether you have had fewer hostile thoughts and feelings. Also evaluate whether the memories you reflect on are better than those of your ordinary days. If so, you might want to live more of your days in this manner.

EXERCISES

1. Describe how pretending today is your last would change the following situations:

   A. Your teenager has woken up on the wrong side of bed. His downcast eyes and monosyllabic communications convey only surliness.

   B. Your spouse has just gotten in the last word, except for the possible rejoinder you can make.

PART **IV**

DEALING WITH HOSTILE PEOPLE

Sometimes you need to determine if the problem is your own hostility or that of someone else. Perhaps that other person is mistreating you. If the other person is too hostile, certainly he or she is mistreating him- or herself. The next section helps you deal with that problem.

"You must be getting tired, dear . . . Do you want me to drive on my own for a while?"

CHAPTER **20**

Help Yourself and/or Others to Change

"Respect yourself and others will respect you."
Confucius,
sixth- and fifth-century B.C. Chinese sage

Reprinted with permission of Doug Marlette and Creators Syndicate.

GENERAL PRINCIPLES

When to Use This Strategy

At this juncture, you may suspect that someone around you has a problem with hostility. This person appears to be on the constant lookout for your misbehavior. Furthermore, you are often the target of that person's ire. If this is true, whatever your own level of hostility, you also have a problem with "secondhand" hostility. A person you care about is engaging in behaviors that may harm *his or her* health. Besides, these experiences definitely lower the quality of *your* life. You are being mistreated and need to protect yourself.

First, explore your suspicion more systematically. In a variation on the Hostility Log (chapter 1), document for a week all occasions in which you are on the receiving end of hostile encounters from other people. Looking over your Log, evaluate what portion of the mistreatment you are receiving is generated by one specific person—a boss, spouse, co-worker, and so on. For each encounter with that someone who is frequently hostile toward you, try to evaluate as honestly as you can by reasoning with yourself (chapter 3) whether *his or her* anger is justified. Remember that it is highly unlikely that you are the one who is incompetent, careless, inconsiderate, or insensitive if most of your hostile encounters are with only this person. If you have warm and satisfying relationships with most of your friends at work and most other people, except for this one unsatisfactory relationship, then *your* hostility is likely not the problem. If you decide it's not you but the other person's hostility that is the problem, you need to learn to cope effectively, or your own health and sense of well-being could be compromised.

How to Use This Strategy

Once you identify someone who frequently treats you badly, evaluate how much you want to stay in the relationship. With people who are relatively unimportant to you, you may want simply to cut back your contact. Get a different roommate next semester, for example. Avoid an irascible neighbor. Reduce your interaction with a troublesome co-worker. Visit a hostile sibling less.

If your tormentor is a more significant figure, explore some other options. If you have a troublesome supervisor, can you transfer to another division of your company you like as well? If your boss owns the company, can you find a comparable or better job elsewhere? (We realize that you may not have the luxury of leaving when your livelihood is at stake.)

For many of us, the most hostile person in our lives is a parent, child, or, most likely of all, a spouse or lover. Improving your relationship is obviously in everyone's best interest! Here are the steps we recommend to deal with a hostile person who is very important to you.

DEALING WITH A HOSTILE SPOUSE OR LIFE PARTNER

You must first realize that you are not the primary problem. You need to understand that *you* are not at fault. Liberate yourself from accepting your partner's view of you as incompetent, careless, inconsiderate, or insensitive. The hostile person's outbursts grow out of his or her own problems with trust, not your behavior. You will need to remind yourself of this anew every day. This perspective may feel uncomfortable at first, and you will almost certainly back-slide on occasion. Persevere.

In dealing with a hostile person, practicing empathy can be useful but very tricky. On the one hand, by understanding that your partner's anger has deep origins in a difficult past or a biological inheritance, you can reinforce your awareness that *your* behavior is not the problem.

On the other hand, you want to avoid becoming *too* accepting while being understanding. Once you're aware where the problem lies, limit your empathy to short-term considerations. Never excuse a partner's misbehavior as acceptable, even given his or her difficult past or biological predisposition.

Always give your partner a chance to empathize with you: "Yes, I haven't taken out the garbage yet. I understand how that would be upsetting. Maybe you'll be less upset when I tell you that I was late getting home because of a traffic jam."

As another step in protecting yourself, carefully review the assertion skills described in chapter 8. These are the most useful tools you possess for dealing with hostile people.

Keeping a record of hostility directed against you will help you become more sensitive to hostile attacks. Be on the lookout for new incidents. Each time you are aware of feeling attacked:

- Describe to your partner the *specific observable behavior.* For example, "Redford, you have just arrived home and are immediately butting into my preparations for dinner. I have planned the menu, shopped, and fixed the vegetables. Now you are trying to take over broiling the fish, after I have told you on numerous occasions that I prefer to cook fish myself."

- Describe your *feelings* and own them as your responsibility. For example, "This makes me feel undervalued, annoyed, and resentful."

- Ask the other person to help you avoid these feelings by making *specific changes.* For example, "I don't want this to be my first feeling when you come home—or my feeling anytime, for that matter."

- Inform the other person of the *likely consequences* if he or she is unable or unwilling to change that behavior. You must be responsible for your subsequent behavior as clearly as you are responsible for your feelings. Consider your potential actions very carefully, as you may have an initial tendency to be either too timid or too bold. Change is always difficult, and you should at first make the consequences clearly limited, if nonetheless real. Little changes, taken one by one, can still be effective. Together, they can add up to big changes, *if* you are consistent. Begin with consequences you can easily deliver: "If you want me to choose fish for dinner, you must let me cook it, without your helping, hovering, or even looking worried. If the next time we have fish you don't leave me alone about cooking it, I won't choose it again for a month."

Because Redford's inability to trust Virginia to cook "correctly" has been an ongoing theme in our marriage, it's clear that Redford's need to be in control of food preparation—to trust Virginia to take care of him—isn't a characteristic easily eradicated once and for all. Years ago, he would become resentful if his efforts to help had been thwarted. For us this represents hard-earned progress. Now, at least we are on the same team. For example: "Gosh, honey, I don't want you to feel unappreciated. I think you're a good cook. Most of all, I want us to have a good time together."

Virginia still isn't pleased with Redford's deep need to be in control of cooking, but at least she no longer takes it personally. She always requests different behavior from him when she feels that he is undervaluing her. Because he is cooperative, really wants to change, and has made a lot of progress, it's a manageable problem.

In addition to protecting yourself against a hostile person who is important to you, you may need to take steps to insure that your life has an overall positive focus.

One effective action you can take is to elicit support from others. Look outside the troubled relationship so that you are less dependent on a person you can't count on to treat you well. Eventually the relationship could be satisfying enough to meet many of your needs, but in the meantime, try to get your main support from other sources. You may want to think of this as a kind of time out.

- Do what you can to achieve satisfaction in your job.

- Develop several other close friendships.

- Reconsider community service (chapter 12), which offers many opportunities for warm interpersonal contacts and feeling appreciated.

You may be willing to tolerate a less-than-satisfactory intimate relationship temporarily, but you also want to be able to look forward to the day when the relationship will be good. Therefore, *insist* on progress. Here you need to affirm both your positive feelings for your partner and your insistence on being treated decently. You are in this relationship because you value your life together. Let your partner hear this often.

Your love is not enough, however. For the partnership to be a healthy one, your partner must also love you effectively. This means being flexible, open to modifying behavior, and willing to practice the strategies for reducing cynicism, angry thoughts, and aggressive acts. If your partner is unwilling to acknowledge his or her hostility or to do the work necessary to change, this unwillingness may be an insurmountable barrier to a satisfying relationship.

Continue to keep your Log about incidents in which you are the target of your partner's hostility. Note if he or she continues frequently to place blame on you, even after you have made quite specific requests using assertion. If after a month or so there is no progress, reevaluate your situation and consider new options.

Should you and your partner as a couple seek out a mental-health professional? Suppose you feel—based on what you have learned in this book—that at least some of the problems in your relationship are due to your partner's hostility. Despite all your efforts to apply what we have suggested, the problems have not abated. In this case you might logically conclude that this is a job for a professional and suggest that the two of you consult a counselor—psychiatrist, social worker, psychologist, member of the clergy—with training in helping couples.

If your partner agrees, well and good. Off you go, and with outside help you can begin to make progress. But what if, as is all too often the case, your partner refuses? Again you can apply what you have learned about assertion: "I have loved you for a long time and think I still do, but something wrong in our relationship is diluting the positive feelings I used to have. I have tried to pinpoint the problem and work with you to fix it, but I'm still unhappy. I have asked you to come with me to see a counselor in hopes of making better progress.

When you refuse even to go see a counselor, it makes me feel trapped and without any hope of improving our relationship. Therefore, I really need to have you agree to come with me to see the counselor for at least a few visits, to try to identify ways we can work on our problems. If you can do this, I will try to do my part to help solve the problems in our relationship. If you continue to refuse, I will be forced to conclude that you are incapable of even trying to work on our problems. In that case, I will leave."

If you do all this and your partner still refuses to budge, or if you go to a counselor but there is still no progress, you may have no choices but to accept things as they are, or leave.

REDUCING HOSTILITY IN OTHER RELATIONSHIPS

Raising a child involves the only relationship in which your commitment to the other person is irrevocable. You cannot walk away from a child who is dependent on you. So if your child is treating you in a hostile manner—as often happens during adolescence—you must take action to repair the relationship. If the strategies described above don't work, you might want to consider professional counseling—for your child alone or as a family.

With a hostile parent, should you cut back on the amount of contact? (Consider seeking counseling yourself, as working through this may help you in all other interactions.)

Why This Strategy Works

In coping with your hostile partner, you are exploring options in stages, beginning with the simplest and most generous. First you are identifying exactly the problem, then asserting yourself. You are seeking professional help if you need it. If nothing succeeds, you have the ultimate option of leaving—unless, of course, we're talking about your relationship with your child. In all cases, you are giving the relationship its best chance for turning into a good one.

For a very evocative portrayal of how a marriage can evolve when one partner does not confront the hostility of the other, we suggest you rent from your video store *Mr. and Mrs. Bridge,* a 1991 movie starring Paul Newman and Joanne Woodward.

Mr. Bridge is a hostile, controlling husband to whom Mrs.

Bridge defers in every case, often at the expense of her own well-being or that of their children. In one scene, for example, his stubborn determination to stay in the country club dining room and finish his dinner nearly causes their death or serious injury when a tornado passes perilously close.

By the end of the film, you will have seen how the lives of Mr. and Mrs. Bridge turn out. As you view this film, think how the outcome could have been different—both for the family's happiness and for Mr. Bridge's health—if Mrs. Bridge had been able to take effective steps to help Mr. Bridge recognize and deal with his hostility.

Our own marriage has evolved more successfully. About fifteen years ago, Virginia insisted that Redford see a counselor in the hope that he would treat her and the children better. Although she implied that she would leave if he didn't go to the counselor, she fully expected him to comply with her request before she made it, as they had talked about this before and he had been receptive to seeking professional help.

Redford's behavior improved somewhat after four years of psychoanalysis, but Virginia still thought he was often hostile and isolated. She was very unhappy.

Virginia then saw a counselor herself about her marriage and problems with a couple of professors at graduate school. Most of her therapy consisted of her describing to her therapist negative incident after negative incident from her marriage. She could have expressed her feelings much more effectively at the time of the incidents, but instead they had festered into an ever-present resentment. In relating all the tribulations from her marriage, she was really hoping to get permission from herself and her therapist to leave Redford.

Virginia's push toward leaving was matched by Redford's redoubled efforts to be less hostile and more connected. This, as well as her psychotherapy, helped her to redouble her efforts at assertion. Gradually, we turned the corner.

Practicing hostility control and assertion usually required a lot of effort, but we made slow but steady progress. We learned what succeeded and what didn't, and our strategies became more effective. Best of all, love blossomed anew. We again became each other's best friend and started enjoying each other's company very much. Over time, our commitment to each other became deeper and more abiding.

Nothing else in our lives has ever rewarded us as handsomely as these efforts to change ourselves and each other. We like to tell our friends that we are now on our third marriage, and it's the best one yet!

Your personal life can also improve if you will commit yourself to making whatever changes are necessary to achieve that goal.

THE ABCS OF HELPING YOURSELF OR ANOTHER TO CHANGE

A. Get out of easily terminated troublesome relations.

B. Realize that you are not at fault when you aren't. Practice assertion.

C. Get support from outside the troubled relationship, including professional help as needed. Insist on progress. If it doesn't come, take all actions necessary to prevent your continued mistreatment.

EXERCISES

1. Consider how you could react in the following situations:

> **A.** You are driving the family car. You've never had an accident, and you have few tickets for traffic violations. Nonetheless, your passenger keeps up a steady flow of traffic information and driving suggestions.

> **B.** Your housemate hovers over you as you cook, repair the sink, or whatever. After you do most of the work, your housemate suggests a way the project can be improved, a suggestion you think will impede rather than improve the project.

> **C.** Your confidant again interrupts you halfway through your sentence.

2. Additional help is available for couples who want to go beyond controlling hostility to making an already good marriage better. If the idea appeals to you, explore the retreats, growth groups, and couple-communication programs available through churches and other organizations in your area. The Association of Couples for Marriage Enrichment (ACME), P.O. Box 10596, Winston-Salem,

NC 27108 (address: 502 North Broad Street, Winston-Salem, NC 27101, telephone, 800-634-8325), may be able to help direct you. Do not be held back by financial considerations, as most of these groups are inexpensive.

EPILOGUE:

Your Last Act

"... any man's death diminishes me,
because I am involved in Mankinde;
And therefore never send to know for
whom the bell tolls; It tolls for thee."
　　　　John Donne,
　　　　　　seventeenth-century English divine

Transport yourself by means of your imagination across decades into your future. You and the people you grew up with have lived through youth, young adulthood, middle age, and senior years. Most of them, after reaching an average life span, have died. You have lived on. Gradually your eyesight, hearing, energy, voice, and mind have faded, and now you are in the hospital, soon to die.

Your spouse visits every day and stays in the reclining chair many nights. (If you have no spouse, bring along your confidant.) What do the two of you talk about? Is it understood that you love each other? Do you have wonderful remembrances to share? The birthday cake the baking powder got left out of and how everyone laughed over the pancake with candles. The thrill of your first child. The other babies looked like wrinkled old men; your baby was beautiful, perfect in every way. Remember the week on the Gulf

Coast when you ate fresh fish every night? The fight you had over the Equal Rights Amendment and how you resolved your differences? How you decided whether to have a TV in the bedroom? (Small TV, earphones.)

Will you remember the delicious physical delights of your youth, that Wednesday afternoon on the cool moss in the deep woods with the sun rays striking down through the oak trees, lighting each other and your hearts?

Remember the thrill of your first grandchild. Remember how menopause required whole new sensitivities and adjustments to more subtle sexual feelings, a triumph of effort for both of you. Remember the wildflowers you both grew for the natural botanical gardens.

Remember the scholarship funds at your high schools you both contributed toward. The shared times in the soup kitchen. Your work to reduce the need for soup kitchens. Your own good fortune and heartfelt good feelings about that.

Are your children there for your exit? Have they bothered to come the long distances so that they can see you once more and tell you that they love you? What do they reminisce about? The 3:00 A.M. leg rubs you gave them when they woke up in the middle of the night with leg aches. How you would braid their hair into long plaits, being careful not to pull. Your running behind their first two-wheeler, steadying the fearful voyager. The trips to the dentist. The help with the math homework. Calling Spanish vocabulary words over and over. Playing pitch and catch. Over and over. Do you see yourself in your children? Are you proud of what you see?

A vase of yellow flowers rests on your bedside table, next to the hospital tissues. Did you ever learn to smell the jonquils? Which did you notice first, the jonquils or the scratchy tissues?

Your best friends—those who are left—hobble in to see you. Will your friends genuinely miss you? Do you often know what your friend is thinking before he or she says it? Are you not embarrassed to say how much you've meant to each other?

Your grandchildren also visit. Did they come because their parents insisted or because you are one of their favorite persons? Are you leaving them with memories of you that will give them courage and acceptance when they inexorably arrive at their own deathbeds?

Ask yourself, are you and the important people in your life sharing an odyssey *right now* that will become memories like these?

Will you and your significant other have such wonderful memories when your ends come?

No matter how you live, eventually you will die. By controlling your aggression, anger, and cynicism, by other good health habits, by luck and good genes, you may delay your end. This may or may not be a destiny you can steer.

You have some control over the kind of life you will look back on in your final hours. Each day of your life, don't let your initial angry or cynical reactions prevent you from moving on to a more positive focus. If you choose to work at it, you can enjoy a life with less hostility and more heartfelt happiness.

NOTES

INTRODUCTION: **Anger Kills**

P. xiv Redford Williams, *The Trusting Heart: Great News About Type A Behavior* (New York: Times Books/Random House, 1989).

P. xvi Virginia Parrott Williams, *Surrealism, Quantum Philosophy and World War I* (New York: Garland Press, 1987).

P. xvi "Before beginning . . . expressing anger." For a bibliography of studies about consequences of expressing anger, see Suzanne M. Retzinger, *Violent Emotions: Shame and Rage in Marital Quarrels* (Newbury Park, Calif.: Sage, 1991). She lists some sources which conclude that expression of anger is likely to lead to further anger as well as others which posit that expression of anger results in well-being for the self and the relationship. For a contrast to our work, see Carol Zisowitz Stearns and Peter N. Stearns, *Anger: The Struggle for Emotional Control in America's History* (Chicago: University of Chicago Press, 1986). One a psychiatrist and the other an historian, these authors assume a considerable constancy for the biological component of anger and express concern that suppression of anger affects emotional spontaneity and moral indignation.

P. xvi–xvii "Myth #1 . . . other behavior." Carol Tavris, *Anger: The Misunderstood Emotion,* rev. ed. (New York: Simon and Schuster, 1989), chapter 5.

CHAPTER 1: **Am I at Risk?**

P. 3–4 "And in a study . . . at all." John C. Barefoot, Kenneth A. Dodge, Bercedis L. Peterson, W. Grant Dahlstrom, and Redford B. Williams, "The Cook-Medley Hostility Scale: Item Content and Ability to Predict Survival," 51 *Psychosomatic Medicine* (1989), 46–57.

CHAPTER 2: **The Facts About Hostility**

P. 30 "This study . . . rates" Ray H. Rosenman, Richard J. Brand, C. David Jenkins, Meyer Friedman, R. Strauss, and M. Wurm, "Coronary Heart Disease in the Western Collaborative Group Study: Final Follow-up Experience of 8½ Years," 233 *Journal of the American Medical Association* (1975), 872–77.

P. 31 "Publication . . . ever before." See Meyer Friedman and Ray H. Rosenman, *Type A Behavior and Your Heart* (New York: Knopf, 1974) for a review of the early research on Type A behavior.

P. 33 "His findings . . . Type A." James A. Blumenthal, Redford B. Williams, Y. Kong, Saul M. Schanberg, and Larry W. Thompson, "Type A Behavior Pattern and Coronary Atherosclerosis," 58 *Circulation* (1978), 634–39.

P. 33 ". . . two other research groups . . . coronary angiography." K. A. Frank, S. S. Heller, Donald S. Kornfeld, A. A. Sporne, and M. B. Weiss, "Type A Behavior Pattern and Coronary Angiographic Findings," 240 *Journal of the American Medical Association* (1978), 761–63; and Steven J. Zyzanski, C. David Jenkins, Thomas J. Ryan, A. Flessas, and M. Everist, "Psychological Correlates of Coronary Angiographic Findings," 136 *Archives of Internal Medicine* (1975), 1234–37.

P. 33 "Indeed, this was exactly the conclusion . . . coronary disease." The Review Panel on Coronary-Prone Behavior and Coronary Heart Disease, "Coronary-Prone Behavior and Coronary Heart Disease: A Critical Review," 63 *Circulation* (1981), 1199–1215.

P. 34 "When we examined . . . younger patients." Redford B. Williams, John C. Barefoot, Thomas L. Haney, Frank E. Harrell, James A. Blumenthal, David B. Pryor, and Bercedis L. Peterson, "Type A Behavior and Angiographically Documented Coronary Atherosclerosis in a Sample of 2,289 Patients," 50 *Psychosomatic Medicine* (1988), 139–52.

P. 34 "The second observation . . . Type A men." Richard B. Shekelle, S. Hulley, J. Neaton, J. Billings, N. Borhani, T. Gerace, D. Jacobs, N. Lasser, Maury Mittlemark, Jeremiah Stamler, and the MRFIT Research Group, "The MRFIT Behavioral Pattern Study: II. Type A Behavior Pattern and Incidence of Coronary Heart Disease," 122 *American Journal of Epidemiology* (1985), 559–70.

P. 35 "The results . . . Type A scores." Redford B. Williams, Thomas L. Haney, Kerry L. Lee, Y. Kong, James A. Blumenthal, and Robert Whalen, "Type A Behavior, Hostility, and Coronary Atherosclerosis," 42 *Psychosomatic Medicine* (1980), 539–49.

P. 35 "He had collected . . . twenty-year period." Richard B. Shekelle, M. Gale, Adrian M. Ostfeld, and Oglesby Paul, "Hostility, Risk of Coronary Disease and Mortality," 45 *Psychosomatic Medicine* (1983), 219–28.

P. 35–36 "The second portent . . . late 1950s." John C. Barefoot, W. Grant Dahlstrom, and Redford B. Williams, "Hostility, CHD Incidence, and Total Mortality: A 25-year Follow-up Study of 255 Physicians," 45 *Psychosomatic Medicine* (1983), 59–63.

P. 37 "Dr. Dahlstrom . . . the 1950s." See citation for chapter one, page 4.

P. 37 ". . . Dr. Edward McCranie . . . health problems." E. McCranie, L. Watkins, J. Brandsma, and B. Sisson, "Hostility, Coronary Heart Disease (CHD) Incidence and Total Mortality: Lack of Association in a 25-Year Follow-Up Study of 478 Physicians," 9 *Journal of Behaviorial Medicine* (1986), 119.

P. 38 "Gloria Leon . . . the MCG doctors study." G. R. Leon, S. E. Finn, D. M. Murray, and J. M. Bailey, "Inability to Predict Cardiovascular Disease from Hostility Scores or MMPI items Related to Type A Behavior, 56 *Journal of Consulting Clinical Psychology* (1988), 596.

P. 38 "A third negative study . . . middle-aged folks." M. D. Hearn, D. M. Murray, and R. V. Luepker, "Hostility, Coronary Heart Disease, and Total Mortality: A 33-Year Follow-Up Study of University Students, 12 *Journal of Behavioral Medicine* (1989), 105.

P. 39 "Because the interviews . . . hostility . . . into account." Michael Hecker, Margaret Chesney, George Black, and N. Frautschi, "Coronary-Prone Behaviors in the Western Collaborative Group Study," 50 *Psychosomatic Medicine* (1988), 153–64; Theodore M. Dembroski, James M. MacDougall, Paul T. Costa, and Gregory A. Grandits, "Antagonistic Hostility as a Predictor of Coronary Heart Disease in the Multiple Risk Factor Intervention Trial," 51 *Psychosomatic Medicine* (1989), 514–22.

P. 39 "Nevertheless, what information . . . similar pattern." See last citation for page 35, this chapter; John C. Barefoot, Ilene C. Siegler, John B. Nowlin, Bercedis L. Peterson, Thomas L. Haney, and Redford B. Williams, "Suspiciousness, Health, and Mortality: A Follow-up Study of 500 Older Adults," 49 *Psychosomatic Medicine* (1987), 450–57.

P. 40, 41 "Timothy Smith . . . social support . . . Smith reports . . . women." ". . . hostile people . . . families." "In a study at a financial . . . work relationships." Timothy W. Smith, Mary Katherine Pope, Jill D. Sanders, Kenneth D. Allred, and Jennifer O'Keefe, "Cynical Hostility at Home and Work: Psychosocial Vulnerability Across Domains," 22 *Journal of Research in Personality* (December 1988), 524–48.

P. 40–41 "Similar results . . . they married." David Mace, *Love and Anger in Marriage* (Grand Rapids, Mich.: Zondervan, 1982).

P. 41 "Everyone agrees . . . widely documented." Alice Miller, *For Your Own Good: Hidden Cruelty in Child-rearing and the Roots of Violence,* trans. Hildegarde and Hunter Hannum (New York: Farrar, Straus & Giroux, 1983).

P. 41 "In another study . . . underutilized." B. Kent Houston and Karen E. Kelly, "Hostility in Employed Women: Relation to Work and Marital Experiences, Social Support, Stress, and Anger Expression," 15 *Personality and Social Psychology Bulletin* (June 1989), 175–82.

P. 41 "From his studies . . . exacerbating conflicts." Timothy W. Smith, "Interactions, Transactions and Type A Pattern: Additional Avenues in the Search for Coronary-Prone Behavior." In *In Search of Coronary-Prone Behavior: Beyond Type A,* ed. Aron W. Siegman and Theodore M. Dembroski (Hillsdale, N.J.: Lawrence Erlbaum, 1989), 91–116.

P. 42 "Meyer Friedman . . . urban populations." Meyer Friedman and

Diane Ulmer, *Treating Type A Behavior—and Your Heart* (New York: Knopf, 1984), 81–82.

P. 44 "Dr. George Kaplan . . . groups." Lisa F. Berkman and Lester Breslow, *Health and Ways of Living: The Alameda County Study* (New York: Oxford University Press, 1983).

P. 44 "Dr. Dan Blazer . . . levels of satisfaction." Dan G. Blazer, "Social Support and Mortality in an Elderly Community Population," 115 *American Journal of Epidemiology* (1982), 684–94.

P. 44 "Along with colleagues . . . underlying heart condition." Redford B. Williams, Robert M. Califf, John C. Barefoot, Thomas L. Haney, William B. Saunders, David B. Pryor, Mark A. Hlatky, Ilene C. Siegler, and Daniel B. Mark, "Prognostic Importance of Social and Economic Resources Among Medically Treated Patients with Angiographically Documented Coronary Artery Disease," 267 *Journal of the American Medical Association* (1992), 520–24.

P. 44 "Among persons living . . . in their urine." R. Fleming, A. Baum, M. M. Giariel, R. J. Gatchel, "Mediating Influences of Social Support on Stress at Three Mile Island," 8 *Journal of Human Stress* (1982), 14–22.

P. 45 ". . . James Pennebaker . . . blood pressure." James W. Pennebaker, *Opening Up: The Healing Power of Confiding in Others* (New York: William Morrow and Co., 1990), 60.

P. 45 "In 1982 . . . cortisal." Redford B. Williams, James D. Lane, Cynthia M. Kuhn, William Melosh, Alice D. White, and Saul M. Schanberg, "Type A Behavior and Elevated Physiological and Neuroendocrine Responses to Cognitive Tasks," 218 *Science* (1982), 483–85.

P. 46–47 "This study . . . blood pressure of nonhostile persons." Edward C. Suarez and Redford B. Williams, "Situational Determinants of Cardiovascular and Emotional Reactivity in High and Low Hostile Men," 51 *Psychosomatic Medicine* (1989), 404–18.

P. 47–48 "For example . . . low Ho scores." Larry D. Jamner, David Shapiro, Iris B. Goldstein, and R. Huy, "Ambulatory Blood Pressure in Paramedics: Effects of Cynical Hostility and Defensiveness," 53 *Psychosomatic Medicine* (1991), 393–406.

P. 48–49 "Among middle-aged men . . . adrenaline responses diminished." Edward C. Suarez, Redford B. Williams, Cynthia M. Kuhn, Eugene Zimmerman, and Saul M. Schanberg, "Biobehavioral Basis of Coronary-Prone Behaviors in Middle-aged Men. Part II: Serum Cholesterol, the Type A Behavior Pattern, and Hostility as Interactive Modulators of Physiological Reactivity," 53 *Psychosomatic Medicine* (1991), 529–37.

P. 49 "The arteries of Egyptian . . . arteriosclerotic lesions." Eileen M. Mikat, Jay M. Weiss, Saul M. Schanberg, Jorge V. Bartolome, Donald B. Hackel, and Redford B. Williams, "Development of Atherosclerotic-like Lesions in the Sand Rat," 1 *Coronary Artery Disease* (1990), 469–76.

P. 49 "In a second study . . . the diet." Eileen M. Mikat, Jorge V. Bartolome, Jay M. Weiss, Saul M. Schanberg, Cynthia M. Kuhn, and Redford B. Williams, "Chronic Norepinephrine Infusion Accelerates Atherosclerotic Lesion Development in Sand Rats Maintained on a High Cholesterol Diet," 53 *Psychosomatic Medicine* (1991), 211.

P. 50–51 "In a series of studies . . . weaker PNS reflex in the Type A's." Motoyasu Muranaka, Hirakazu Monou, Jinichi Suzuki, James D. Lane, Norman B. Anderson, Cynthia M. Kuhn, Saul M. Schanberg, Nancy McCown, and Redford B. Williams, "Physiological Responses to Catecholamine Infusions in Type A and Type B Men," 7 (Suppl) *Health Psychology* (1988), 145–63; Shin Fukudo, James D. Lane, Norman B. Anderson, Cynthia M. Kuhn, Saul M. Schanberg, Nancy McCown, Motoyasu Muranaka, Jinichi Suzuki, and Redford B. Williams, "Accentuated Vagal Antagonism of Beta-adrenergic Effects on Ventricular Repolarization: Differential Responses Between Type A and B men." In press *Circulation* (1992).

P. 51 "It is quite interesting . . . exam periods." J. Scanlan, M. Laudenslager, M. Boccia, et al., "Anger Expression and Hostility: Effects on Natural Cytotoxicity and Plasma Lipids in Medical Students." In press *Psychosomatic Medicine* (1992).

P. 53 "Under the direction . . . to consume more caffeine." Ilene C. Siegler, Bercedis L. Peterson, John C. Barefoot, Redford B. Williams, "Hostility During Late Adolescence Predicts Coronary Risk Factors at Midlife." In press *American Journal of Epidemiology* (1992).

P. 53 "Dr. Larry Scherwitz . . . participants." Larry W. Scherwitz, L. L. Perkins, Margaret A. Chesney, G. H. Hughes, S. Sidney, and T. A. Manolio, "Cook-Medley Hostility and Detrimental Health Behaviors in Young Adults: The CARDIA Study." In press *American Journal of Epidemiology* (1992).

P. 54 "Research on . . . including hostility." Timothy W. Smith, M. McGonigle, C. W. Turner, M. H. Ford, and M. L. Slattery, "Cynical Hostility in Monozygotic Male Twins," 53 *Psychosomatic Medicine* (1991), 684–92.

P. 55–56 "By feeding cats . . . the heart." Richard L. Verrier, "Neurochemical Approaches to the Prevention of Ventricular Fibrillation," 45 *Federation Proceedings* (1986), 2191–96.

P. 56 "Dr. Bonnie Spring . . . gaining weight." Bonnie Spring, paper presented at the annual meeting of the American College of Neuropsychopharmacology, San Juan, Puerto Rico, Dec. 1991.

P. 56 "Finally, reduced . . . more alcohol." James Ballenger, Frederick K. Goodwin, L. Frank Major, G. L. Brown, "Alcohol and Central Serotonin Metabolism in Man," 36 *Archives of General Psychiatry* (1979), 224–27.

P. 56 "A strain of rats . . . but no less water." W. J. McBride, L. Murphy, L. Lumeng, and T. K. Li, "Effects of Ro 15-4513, Fluoxetine and Desipramine on the Intake of Ethanol, Water and Food by the Alcohol-Preferring (P) and -Nonpreferring (NP) Lines of Rats," 30 *Pharmacology, Biochemistry and Behavior* (1988), 1045–50.

P. 58 "Dr. Meyer Friedman . . . heart problems." Meyer Friedman et al., "Alteration of Type A Behavior and Its Effect on Cardiac Recurrences in Post-Myocardial Infarction Patients: Summary Results of the Recurrent Coronary Prevention Project," 112 *American Heart Journal* (1986), 653–59.

P. 58–59 "More recently, Dr. Dean Ornish . . . program's success." Dean Ornish, *Dr. Dean Ornish's Program for Reversing Heart Disease* (New York: Random House, 1990).

P. 59 "In a Montreal . . . salutary effects." Nancy Frasure-Smith and R. Prince, "The Ischemic Heart Disease Life Stress Monitoring Program: Impact on Mortality," 47 *Psychosomatic Medicine* (1985), 431–45.

P. 59–60 "Equally encouraging . . . care group." David Spiegel, J. R. Bloom, H. C. Kraemer, and E. Gottheil, "Effect of Psychosocial Treatment on Survival of Patients with Metastatic Breast Cancer," 2 *Lancet* (1989), 888–90.

PART III: SURVIVAL SKILLS

P. 61 "Your attitudes . . . these qualities." Suzanne C. Kobasa, "Stressful Life Events, Personality, and Health: An Inquiry into Hardiness," 37 *Journal of Personality and Social Psychology* (1979), 1–11; Suzanne C. Kobasa, Salvatore R. Maddi, and Stephen Kahn, "Hardiness and Health: A Prospective Study," 42 *Journal of Personality and Social Psychology* (1982), 168–77.

CHAPTER 4: Stop Hostile Thoughts, Feelings, and Urges

P. 77 "In his concept . . . the 'tribe.' " Robert Ornstein, *Multimind: A New Way of Looking at Human Behavior* (Boston: Houghton Mifflin, 1986).

P. 78 Robert Louis Stevenson, *The Strange Case of Dr. Jekyll and Mr. Hyde* (Lincoln, Neb.: University of Nebraska Press, 1990), 123.

CHAPTER 6: Meditate

P. 89 This is for breathing meditation. Yoga has different effects. "Meditators . . . passive victim." David M. Wulff, *Psychology of Religions: Classic and Contemporary Views* (New York: Wiley, 1991), 172–84; Kenneth R. Pelletier, *Mind as Healer, Mind as Slayer: A Holistic Approach to Preventing Stress Disorders* (New York: Delta, 1977), 192–93.

CHAPTER **8: Assert Yourself**

P. 101 "In face-to-face . . . *nonverbal:* . . ." Janet S. St. Lawrence, "Assessment of Assertion." In *Progress in Behavior Modification,* ed. Michel Hersen, Richard Eisler, and Peter Miller. V.21 (Newbury Park, Calif.: Sage, 1987), 165–66.

P. 102 "Make a simple assertion." See Arthur J. Lange and Patricia Jakubowski, *Responsible Assertive Behavior: Cognitive/Behavioral Procedures for Trainers* (Champaign, Ill.: Research Press, 1976), 13–21, 33–34 for a listing of assertion types. Our list of options is different from theirs but takes its inspiration from them.

P. 105 "If you are angry . . . avoid secrets." Harriet Goldhor Lerner, *The Dance of Anger: A Woman's Guide to Changing the Patterns of Intimate Relationships* (New York: Harper & Row, 1985), chapters 5, 6, and 9.

P. 109 "Childhood mortality rates . . . injury-related deaths." T. Berry Brazelton and Edward Zigler, "Foreword." In Bret C. Williams and C. Arden Miller, *Preventive Health Care for Young Children: Findings from a 10-Country Study and Directions for United States Policy* (National Center for Clinical Infant Programs, 2000 14th Street North, Suite 380, Arlington, Va., 1991), 1.

CHAPTER **9: Care for a Pet**

P. 111–112 "A large series . . . 86 minutes." Aaron Honori Katcher and Alan M. Beck, "Animal Companions: More Companion than Animal." In *Man and Beast Revisited,* ed. Michael H. Robinson and Lionel Tiger (Washington: Smithsonian, 1991), 267.

P. 114 "Also, contact . . . modern age." Leo K. Bustad, "Man and Beast Interface: An Overview of Our Interrelationships." In *Man and Beast Revisited,* 243.

P. 114–115 "In his book . . . actually decreased." James J. Lynch, *The Language of the Heart: The Body's Response to Human Dialogue* (New York: Basic Books, 1985). See also Leo K. Bustad, "Man and Beast Interface: An Overview of Our Relationships." In *Man and Beast Revisited,* 254–55.

P. 115 "Animals also . . . pet as well." James J. Lynch, *The Broken Heart: The Medical Consequences of Loneliness* (New York: Basic Books, 1977), chapter 6, pp. 156–80. As you might expect, early experience, subsequent learning, and genetic predisposition influence the pattern and degree of cardiac response elicited by human contact.

P. 115–116 Jack London, *The Call of the Wild* (New York: Grosset and Dunlap, 1931), 149–51.

P. 117 John Steinbeck, *Travels with Charley in Search of America* (New York: Viking Penguin, 1980; paperback, Penguin Books).

P. 117 T. S. Eliot, *Old Possum's Book of Practical Cats* (New York: Harcourt Brace, 1982), paperbound copy also available.

CHAPTER 10: Listen!

P. 120–121 "Avoid being *judgmental* . . . eventually summarize." William H. Cormier and L. Sherilyn Cormier, *Interviewing Strategies for Helpers: A Guide to Assessment, Treatment and Evaluation* (Belmont, Calif.: Brooks/Cole, 1979), 72–73.

P. 122 "Larry Scherwitz . . . no angina." Larry Scherwitz et al., "Type A Behavior, Self-Involvement and Coronary Atherosclerosis," 45 *Psychosomatic Medicine,* 47–57.

CHAPTER 11: Practice Trusting Others

P. 130 "Navy Commander . . . you've got." *People* (4 February 1991), 39. Also see Jim and Sybil Stockdale, *In Love and War: The Story of a Family's Ordeal and Sacrifice During the Vietnam Years* (New York: Harper & Row, 1984), 402–403.

CHAPTER 12: Take on Community Service

P. 132–133 "Look for situations . . . trying to help." Allan Luks with Peggy Payne, *The Healing Power of Doing Good: The Health and Spiritual Benefits of Helping Others* (New York: Fawcett Columbine, 1991), 113–24, 247.

P. 134 "An experiment conducted . . . experiment began." P. Zimbardo, "The Mind Is a Formidable Jailer: A Pirandellian Prison," *The New York Times Magazine* (8 April 1973) as quoted in John Sabini, "Aggression in the Laboratory." In *Violence: Perspectives on Murder and Aggression,* ed. Irwin L. Kutash et al. (San Francisco: Jossey-Bass, 1978), 368–69.

P. 135 "Twenty-seven hundred . . . clear for women." James S. House, Cynthia Robbins, and Helen Metzner, "The Association of Social Relationships and Activities with Mortality: Prospective Evidence from the Tecumseh Community Health Study," 116 *American Journal of Epidemiology,* 123–40.

P. 135 "Howard Andrews . . . volunteered frequently." Howard Andrews, "Helping and Health: The Relationship between Volunteer Activities and Health-Related Outcomes," 7 *Advances* (1990), 25–34.

P. 135 "Two psychologists . . . was expressed." Karen S. Kendall and Mary Beth Kenkel, "Social Exchange in the Natural Helping Interaction," 10 *Journal of Rural Community Psychology* (1989), 25–45.

P. 135 "The so-called . . . put forth." Eileen Rockefeller Growald and Allan Luks, "Beyond Self: The Immunity of Samaritans," *American Health* (March 1988), 51–53.

CHAPTER 13: Increase Your Empathy

P. 144 "A series . . . to empathize." Shahbaz Mallick and Boyd R. McCandless, "A Study of Catharsis of Aggression," 4 *Journal of Personality and Social Psychology* (December 1966), 591–96.

P. 144 "In another experiment . . . when it occurred." D. Zillman and J. R. Cantor, "Effect of Timing of Information about Mitigating Circumstances on Emotional Responses to Provocation and Retaliatory Behavior," 12 *Journal of Experimental Social Psychology* (1976), 38–55.

CHAPTER **14: Be Tolerant**
P. 152–153 Sophocles, *The Three Theban Plays,* trans. Robert Fagles, Introduction and Notes by Bernard Know (New York: Viking, 1982), lines 776–78 and 788–809, pp. 77–78.

CHAPTER **15: Forgive**
P. 159 "Large-scale grievances . . . from a counselor." Also see first citation for page 41 in chapter two. Unacknowledged anger against a parent is especially troublesome because you may in turn treat your own children in a similar manner. See Alice Miller, *For Your Own Good.*

P. 159 "Solid evidence . . . Type A." Berton H. Kaplan, "Social Health and the Forgiving Heart: The Type B Story," 15 *Journal of Behavioral Medicine* (1992), 3–14.

P. 159 "Richard Fitzgibbons . . . wronged them." Richard Fitzgibbons, "The Cognitive and Emotive Uses of Forgiveness in the Treatment of Anger," 23 *Psychotherapy* (1986), 629–33.

P. 160–161 "More that fifteen . . . to forgive them." Judith Wallerstein and Sandra Blakeslee, *Second Chances: Men, Women and Children a Decade after Divorce* (New York: Ticknor & Fields, 1989), 135.

CHAPTER **16: Have a Confidant**
P. 165 "James Pennebaker . . . in our minds." James W. Pennebaker, *Opening Up: The Healing Power of Confiding in Others* (New York: Morrow, 1990).

P. 165–166 "Nineteen survivors . . . consoled each other." Joel E. Dimsdale, "The Coping Behavior of Nazi Concentration Camp Survivors," 131 *American Journal of Psychiatry* (July 1974), 795.

P. 166–167 Mark Twain, *Adventures of Huckleberry Finn* (New York: Harper & Row, 1987), 271–72.

CHAPTER **17: Laugh at Yourself**
P. 171 For another description of the types of humor, see Barbara Killinger, "Humor in Psychotherapy: A Shift to a New Perspective." In *Handbook of Humor and Psychotherapy: Advances in the Clinical Use of Humor,* ed. William F. Fry Jr. and Waleed A. Salameh (Sarasota, Fla.: Professional Resource Exchange, 1987).

P. 173 *"Exaggeration* is . . . initial exaggeration." Joel Goodman, "How to Get More Smileage Out of Your Life: Making Sense of Humor, Then Serving It." In *Handbook of Humor Research: V 2 Applied Studies,* ed. Paul E. McGhee and Jeffrey H. Goldstein (New York: Springer-Verlag, 1983), 13–15.

P. 173 *"Anticipate* situations . . . old underwear.' " Norman Cousins, *Head First: The Biology of Hope* (New York: Dutton, 1989), 129.

P. 174 "In *Anatomy of* . . . fatal collagen disease." Norman Cousins, *Anatomy of an Illness as Perceived by a Patient* (New York: Norton, 1979), 39–40, 145–50.

P. 174 "Numerous laboratory . . . of aggression." Robert Baron, *Human Aggression* (New York: Plenum, 1977), 263–66.

P. 174 "Studies of the physiology . . . first place." Jeffrey H. Goldstein, "Therapeutic Effects of Laughter." In *Handbook of Humor and Psychotherapy,* 11–15; Paul E. McGhee, "The Role of Arousal and Hemispheric Lateralization in Humor." In *Handbook of Humor Research: V 1 Basic Issues,* ed. Paul E. McGhee and Jeffrey Goldstein (New York: Springer-Verlag, 1983), 13–37.

P. 174–175 "This calming effect . . . start of the study." Barbara Frederickson and Robert Levenson, "Positive Emotions Speed Recovery from Negative Emotional Arousal." Paper submitted for publication, 1992.

P. 175–176 "As reported . . . health had improved." Ronald E. Smith, "The Use of Humor in the Counterconditioning of Anger Responses: A Case Study," 4 *Behavior Therapy* (1973), 576–80.

P. 176–177 "According to the humorist Roger Rosenblatt . . . very long time." *New York Times* (17 November 1991), section 2, p. 5.

CHAPTER 18: **Become More Religious**

P. 182 "In his book . . . fruitful existence." Hans Kung, *Theology for the Third Millennium* (New York: Doubleday, 1988), 244.

P. 182–183 "Gerald Caplan . . . your new place." Gerald Caplan, *Support Systems and Community Mental Health* (New York: Behavioral Publications, 1974), 25–26.

P. 183 "Several studies . . . dietary fat intake." Y. Friedlander, J. D. Kark, and Y. Stein, "Religious Orthodoxy and Myocardial Infarction in Jerusalem—A Case Control Study," 10 *International Journal of Cardiology* (1986), 33–41. Y. Friedlander, J. D. Kark, and Y. Stein, "Religious Observance and Plasma Lipids and Lipoproteins among 17-Year-Old Jewish Residents of Jerusalem," 16 *Preventative Medicine* (1987), 70–79.

P. 183 "In a large-scale . . . church less often." Thomas Graham, Berton H. Kaplan, et al., "Frequency of Church Attendance and Blood Pressure Elevation," 1 *Journal of Behavioral Medicine* (March 1978), 37–43.

P. 183 "In another large . . . not a factor." George W. Comstock and Kay B. Partridge, "Church Attendance and Health," 25 *Journal of Chronic Diseases* (1972), 665–72.

P. 183–184 "The emerging wisdom . . . mentally healthy." *New York Times* (10 September 1991), C–1; Allen E. Bergin, "Values and Religious Issues in Psychotherapy and Mental Health," 45 *American Psychologist* (April 1991), 394–403; David M. Wulff, *Psychology of Religions: Classic and Contemporary Views* (New York: Wiley, 1991), chapter 5.

P. 184 "Jacques Maritain . . . Jacques and Raïssa." Raïssa Maritain, *Les Grandes Amitiés: Souvenirs* (NY: Éditions de la Maison Française, 1941), 92, 101, 112, 114–115, 116–149.

P. 185 "We ask God . . . the Gospel." Jacques Maritain, *Notebooks.* Translated by Joseph W. Evans. (Albany, NY: Magi Books, 1984), 34.

P. 185 "To say that . . . image of God." Jacques Maritain, "The Conquest of Freedom." In *A Maritain Reader,* ed. by Donald and Idella Gallagher. (Garden City, NY: Image Books, 1966), 131.

CHAPTER 19: Pretend Today Is Your Last
P. 191–192 Charles Dickens, *A Christmas Carol* (New York: Pocket Books, 1939).

INDEX

ABOUT THE AUTHORS

REDFORD WILLIAMS, M.D., is director of behavioral research at Duke University Medical Center as well as professor of psychiatry and associate professor of medicine. He did his medical internship at Yale University School of Medicine and did two years of research at NIH. He is the author of *The Trusting Heart* as well as of dozens of scientific papers. He has appeared on many major television shows, including *Good Morning America*. Bill Moyers will be airing a PBS special focusing on Dr. Williams' research, among others, in February 1993. VIRGINIA WILLIAMS, PH.D., is an historian and the author of *Surrealism, Quantum Philosophy and World War I*. The Williamses have been married for over twenty-five years.